Discoveri Christ

Reflections, stories, challenges and prayers from the World Church

Advent and Christmas

Compiled by Maureen Edwards

International Bible Reading Association

Cover photograph: *Safe in His Mother's Arms* – Painting by Wang Hon-yi, Jiangsu, China.

Published by:
International Bible Reading Association
1020 Bristol Road
Selly Oak
Birmingham B29 6LB
Great Britain

ISBN: 0–7197–0989–X

First published: 2000

Designed and typeset by Christian Education Publications

Printed and bound in the UK by Biddles Limited

Contents

Preface

This book is not just for Christmas, though it would make an acceptable Christmas gift. It is a book to be dipped into at times when we have the 'space' which Melvyn Matthews writes about so helpfully in his chapter on prayer. Each chapter takes us on a journey with a companion who knows the territory well and can introduce us to the personal stories of people whose daily experiences may be very different from ours, but who share a common experience when it comes to celebrating Christ's coming into the world. Having met the people, we are then invited to pray with them.

In some cases the journey is to countries overseas. We share with Barbara and David Calvert their recent visit – with a Christian Aid group from Gloucester – to Haiti where they met poverty-stricken people who live with an advent hope of better things to come. In the company of Magali do Nascimento Cunha, a Christian journalist who works among the poor communities of Brazil, we are introduced to a vibrant community in Rio de Janeiro. Though they live beneath the mountain crowned by the statue of Christ the Redeemer, they find his real presence in the streets of the *favelas*. Israel Selvanayagam, a presbyter of the Church of South India, enables us to join in worship with Christians in rural India. Bernard Thorogood, who was for eighteen years a mission partner in Polynesia, invites us to read our Bibles with those who live in the sun-drenched islands of the South Pacific.

Not all the journeys are geographical ones. We are taken by Sheila Cassidy, who works as a specialist in psycho-social oncology, into the world of pain and suffering, to hear how the gospel of the incarnation sounds to those who are terminally ill or who have to watch their loved ones in pain. We are reminded of an African proverb that true friendship is only experienced when we not only eat and laugh together but when we can weep together too.

The book begins and ends with journeys that take us inwards. The first, by Alec Gilmore, a former Director of *Feed the Minds*, takes us into the biblical texts surrounding the story of Christ's coming into the world, and particularly setting them in the context of Old Testament prophecy. The last chapter by Melvyn Matthews, the Canon Chancellor of

Wells Cathedral, takes us into the world of prayer and gives some practical advice as to how we can train ourselves in the practice of prayer, drawing particular examples from the prayers included within the Christmas narratives.

To those who are regular users of *Words For Today*, the IBRA notes on daily Bible readings, our companions on all these journeys have familiar names. One of the great strengths of the IBRA notes is that they always make us feel part of a worldwide family, so it is appropriate that we should invite so many familiar friends to join us as we celebrate Christmas.

Pauline Webb
Former Organiser of Religious Broadcasting
in the BBC World Service

Introduction

The painting by Wang Hon-yi of a Chinese Christ-child and Madonna – on the front cover – symbolises the wonderful way in which artists of each culture see and paint Christ in their own colour and tradition, and against the background of their own natural environment, where trees and flowers are different from those of other parts of the world. We might have chosen an Indian Christ, or an African Christ, or an Aboriginal Christ, and each would be different and special. The Christ who came to be the Saviour of the world is seen with the physical features, clothes and experience of every people in art, poetry, prayer and biblical interpretation. That is what we have sought to show in this book which brings together some of the facets and challenges of Christmas from the Caribbean, India, Latin America, the Pacific and Britain.

In each culture the most challenging insights come from people who are poor, forgotten, and disabled, or from those who serve alongside them. They remind us that the meaning of Christmas lies much deeper than the tinsel and glitter, and that it is not so much about how the poor and frail might benefit from the affluent and strong, but about what the rich can learn from the poor, and the strong from the weak. For Christ himself became poor 'so that by his poverty you might become rich' (2 Corinthians 8.9).

We are also pointed to the reality of darkness in each context – the darkness we tend to gloss over, and the less perceptible space which we either don't see, or hurry to fill with the trivia and clutter of modern life. This darkness and space are as much a part of the meaning of Christmas as the cribs, carols and more celebratory, socially acceptable signs of the festival. Indeed, there are those for whom – in pain, isolation and confusion – Christmas celebrations are a 'hollow mockery'. Christmas is as much a sharing of sorrow as it is of joy, whether we focus on experiences of devastation or poverty in some parts of the world, or the suffering and loneliness of folk nearby in our own city, town or village.

Indeed, we come to see Christ today, 'incarnate', enfleshed, in children eliminated by death squads on the streets of Rio de Janeiro, in children and adults coming to terms with suffering, grief and loss, in Indian babies abandoned because they are female... The Saviour of the world is not often found among the ranks of the affluent and powerful, but among ordinary folk in the villages, the shanty towns, the 'inner city'... And those who love and share and struggle together to create a better future are signs of 'God with us' – God who fills the hungry with good things and raises from among them the leaders for whom they long and pray. The light still shines in the darkness and the darkness has never succeeded in putting it out.

That is why Christmas is a celebration, and ordinary people of every culture – even the poorest – know how to celebrate. I remember, on a visit to the Church of South India, being woken up just after midnight on the first day of Advent by the singing of carols from groups around the Medak compound, rather like what Israel Selvanayagam describes on page 54. And the celebration continued in a variety of places throughout the day. In our seven years of living in Kenya, it was wonderful to be with people who love to put on new clothes for Christmas and who can always make room for one more at their table. And, of course, the various ways and people with whom we have, as a family, shared and celebrated Christmas over the years are memories I treasure.

This book has been written primarily for personal reflection, and for that reason, some prayers have been added at the end of each chapter. We hope that it will be used as part of your preparation for Christmas. I hope you will find much in this book, individually or together in a group, to make you think, insights to weave into your experience, to enrich your life of prayer, and challenges which will change your lives.

Maureen Edwards – Editor

Versions of the Bible

All biblical quotations in this book are taken from *The New Revised Standard Version*, unless otherwise indicated:

AV – *The Authorised Version*

NEB – *The New English Bible*

NJB – *The New Jerusalem Bible*

REB – *The Revised English Bible*

Church's liturgies have related to a selection of prophetic texts as the basis for Advent and the Christmas season, and these have become the main focus for the celebration of Christmas.

The details of the stories have often been questioned. When they came to be written down they were doubtless the subject of considerable expansion as difficulties and inconsistencies were smoothed out and what was omitted or unmentioned was filled in, but they are not to be thought of as the product of a professional 21st century historian working with western presuppositions[3]. Think of them rather as the reflection of an ancient tradition, an indication of the stories about Jesus that came through in the preaching and ministry of the early Church, and whose value lies less in their historical accuracy and more in the truth they convey.

Briefly, they present a picture of Jesus as the Son of David, and show that he was Son of God before the baptismal announcement. They throw light on Joseph by relating him to his Old Testament counterpart who also had dreams and escaped into Egypt, and they never lose sight of the fact that Jesus embodies the whole story of Israel, from Abraham, Sarah and Isaac to John the Baptist, whose parents are carbon copies of Abraham and Sarah[4].

Jesus embodies the whole story of Israel

They provide a gateway to the Jesus of history[5], a real person, in a real world, and as such contain the seeds of a new way of life, even a liberation theology[6], with an option for those without name and without power, like the shepherds, set over against the ruling giants such as the emperor Augustus and the imperial governor Quirinius.

Taken together with John 1.1–14 (and certain other passages), they also form the basis for the doctrine of incarnation (literally – 'enfleshment'). The fourth Gospel speaks of the Word *becoming flesh* and taking on human form. The point is not that Jesus *proclaimed* the Word but that *he* was the Word[7]; 'what God was, the Word was' (verse 1, REB). Everything that was present in God he *embodied* in his own person.

3. Hans Kung, *Credo*, p.45, SCM Press, 1993.
4. Raymond E Brown, 'Infancy Narratives' in R J Coggins & J L Houlden (eds), *A Dictionary of Biblical Interpretation*, pp.311f, SCM Press, 1990.
5. Hans Kung, op. cit., p.47.
6. Hans Kung, op. cit., p.45.
7. The emphasis here is important. John 1.1 is almost universally misread at Christmas as 'The Word *was* God'. The better reading is ' *The Word* was God' as comes through clearly in the *Revised English Bible* with its translation, 'what God was, the Word was'.

The preparation

What the Bible does not do is rush to the end at the expense of the beginning. The preparation for this 'event' took 2000 years and all that led up to it is important. To get to the heart of it we might profitably use more time creating the atmosphere. We can do it in the home, by the way we spend Christmas Eve, or in the church, by the way we order Advent and Christmas services.

To create atmosphere calls for imagination. There is no need to re-create the scene, with Bethlehem, crib, star, and shepherds and wise men in dressing gowns. We are not there, we are here. It is not then, it is now. And just as a little scenery can enhance a drama by leaving something to the imagination, allowing theatre, audience and actors to do the rest, so too much attention to history and 'actuality' can stifle rather than create 'reality'.

One of the first passages to be read in Advent is Isaiah 9.1–7 with 'the people who walked in darkness'. If, in our enthusiasm to get to the light, we short-circuit the darkness, we deprive ourselves of the wonder of the light when it comes. The darkness is important. The yoke may have been broken, but the only people likely to appreciate it are those who were deeply conscious of its pressure. There are signs of peace, but the boots of the warriors and the garments stained with blood cannot be forgotten. And though Isaiah proclaims a solid basis for hope of better things to come, he is careful to emphasise that it is still all in the future. It was then. It is now. It always will be. The coming of Jesus did not change the world overnight. Nor will any celebration of his birth. We live in hope, but it is hope that is born of frustration and failure, pain, suffering and death.

There is a ray of hope with a child who is to be called *Immanuel*, but again it is in the context of a doomed city in a desperate situation, and where there is no sense of despair there is little need for hope (Isaiah 7.10–18). Prerequisites of the Christmas atmosphere therefore are darkness, cold, a sense of the ordinary, and a feeling of being at rock-bottom.

Into this darkness may then break shafts of light, or rays of hope, like walking through a forest glade with rays of sunlight falling intermittently across your path, or sitting in the half light of a gothic cathedral with its tall pillars, and sunlight breaking in through the stained glass windows. Slowly, as the seasons turn, we begin to appreciate the rays

We live in hope, but it is hope that is born of frustration and failure, pain, suffering and death

of hope and warmth in the darkness and the chill of our lives.

Habakkuk 1–2 then offers a useful way of developing the picture presented in Isaiah and adds the notion of silence. Chapter 1 declares the prophet's frustration, irritation and impatience. He feels surrounded by violence and injustice (verses 1–4). Can we look around us until we feel it? He fears the mighty powers and forces that he hears about (verses 5–9). Can we identify them, today? And name them? They seem to be beyond the control of kings, rulers and governments (verses 10–11). Really? Whoever can they be? Where are they? Surely they cannot be allowed to get away with it (verses 12–14).

God responds in chapter 2. Shame them (verses 9–11). Get a grip on yourself and your values (verses 12–17). See these things for what they are (verses 18–19). Then, after a catalogue of woe, and with a minimum of hope that anything is going to change for the better, the climax comes in verse 20 with what Otto[8] describes as 'the numinous silence of sacrament', the realisation that 'God is in the midst'. Beginning with the word 'but', verse 20 marks a distinction from everything that has gone before. It is the dawn of a new age: 'But the Lord is in his holy temple; let all the earth keep silence before him.' Why silence?

Because God's great moment, marking that total change and the dawn of the new age, was in the silence of a dark night when the earth was cold and still, 'frozen hard as iron, water like a stone'. No words. Hardly action. Certainly not the obvious, the familiar, the previously tried and failed, the logical or the expected. On all counts it was the most unlikely to achieve anything in the foreseeable future, even if anyone noticed, which most people didn't.

In that moment of stillness, on a dark night, in a remote spot, he simply put down his baby on the face of the earth and waited to see what happened – the baby to herald the dawn of a new beginning.

God's great moment, marking that total change and the dawn of the new age, was in the silence of a dark night when the earth was cold and still

Renewal

In the coldness of the dark night the new baby is a sign, symbol and seal of renewal. The event changes human beings and transforms relationships. It also changes our attitude to the material world and the universe. In both it is a renewal of values.

8. Otto, *The Idea of the Holy*, pp.216f, Oxford University Press, 1926.

Renewal of human beings

One way of exploring renewal in people is to focus not so much on what they do as on what they feel, not on what happens to them but on how they respond.

At its most rudimentary, the Christmas story gave hope to people without babies: Elizabeth and Zechariah in their old age. Indirectly it gave encouragement, purpose and support to people whose lives were being turned inside out by the arrival of an unplanned, if not entirely unwanted, baby: for Mary and Joseph, a mixture of surprise and joy, tempered by an awareness of forces working beyond themselves, and a call for a considerable adjustment to their lifestyle. In different ways, both families were brought face to face with the impossible and had to work out with God what could be achieved through it.

These experiences and emotions, not always or necessarily connected with babies, are common to humanity the world over. They are the stuff of soap opera. Some in particular take centre stage at Christmas because they are there in the birth narratives, but they also reward exploration in other parts of the Bible.

Barrenness and the frustration and disappointment that go with it are a recurring theme, for example, in Genesis 12–50, beginning with Sarah. An imaginative reading of these stories alongside the birth narratives may bring out other facets that go well beyond the problems of reproduction. There are the feelings of disappointment and guilt that often go with the inability to achieve what you want to achieve and what you know is expected. The pain of being held responsible for something which may not be your fault. The frustration that comes from waiting and hoping, together with the false dawns only to be shattered by yet further disappointment.

With the emotions go the images, and the images extend our horizons. The baby born to the barren woman is the same as the one born in the doomed city which gives hope to the nation (Isaiah 7.14), and the one who again demonstrates God's capacity to handle the unexpected and achieve the impossible when he turns up as a shoot from a stump (Isaiah 11.1).

Once on the wavelength, we begin to see other 'stumps' and other 'shoots' – a new spirit, wisdom and righteousness, justice for the poor and equity for the meek. People are being changed. Nature is being changed – the

Barrenness and the frustration and disappointment that go with it are a recurring theme

wolf, the lamb, the leopard, the kid, and so on. And all because of that child (Isaiah 11.1–9).

Ezekiel then moves the scene into the wilderness with that picture of a man gazing over a valley of dry bones (37.1–14). A different kind of barrenness. The same emotions – waiting, hoping, despairing – but in a different context. And as the child transforms the barren woman and all around her, so new life suddenly transforms the valley and its surroundings.

Next comes John the Baptist, 'a voice crying in the wilderness'. Why in the wilderness? Why such a lone voice? Why was nobody listening? Why did many of his hearers not like what he said? Even with a few followers he was still a tiny minority. So where is the wilderness and where is John the Baptist in our society today? Who is listening to him? Who is drowning him? Answers to these questions in the kind of atmosphere created at the beginning may send ripples far and wide.

'The baby' is the source of all our dreams and aspirations, whether it be the Jews waiting for the Messiah, Christians waiting for Christmas, or two tramps 'waiting for Godot'. We are all wanting, waiting and hoping. Then, one day, something happens, and 'the baby' is the beginning of fulfilment. The season is changing. Hope is born. Renewal is on the way, and there are no limits to its agenda.

Renewal of the earth

'Comfort ye, comfort ye...' (Isaiah 40.1–11, AV) is another of the more familiar Christmas readings, thanks perhaps as much to Handel as to Isaiah. Just as earlier we had to get behind the darkness, so now we have to get beyond the comfort. New beginnings are fine but only if we recognise what has to be done beforehand. We are to 'prepare the way' and 'make a highway'. Not just plans, but action. Not just ideas, but creativity. We don't have to move the earth. God will do those things we cannot do, but we do have to make a start.

How? What does it mean in today's world to 'prepare the way' for the coming of the Kingdom?

Isaiah 35, that great poem on renewal often read at Christmas, offers some clues, but it may offer more if it is read with the previous chapter which points the contrast. Chapter 34 thrusts us into wilderness – a world neglected, physically unattractive and unpleasant to live in (verses 2–4), marred by violence and self-interest (verses 5–7),

'The baby' is the source of all our dreams and aspirations

reverting to wilderness and refusing to respond to treatment for renewal (verses 7–17). Chapter 35 offers a wilderness that blossoms. 34.9–10 has a land that is burned and acid; 35.6–7 has one where water, streams and pools break out everywhere. Between the two there is no natural connection. One does not lead automatically into the other. Somebody has to 'prepare the way'.

Chapter 35 is sometimes read as an image of the exiles returning from Babylon and looking hopefully to a new future (verses 1–4), and there is no shortage of people like that in the world. Sometimes it is seen as a foreshadowing of the life of Jesus where the eyes are opened, the ears unstopped and the lame walk (especially verses 5–6), and there are plenty of people seeking to prepare the way by exercising that kind of ministry. Sometimes it is thought of simply as a dream of an ideal world we are never likely to see, where the worst hazards are contained if not controlled (verses 8–10). But on any interpretation the two chapters move us forward from the darkness and the cold, where we began, to the rustle of spring and the realisation of our dreams.

Isaiah 34 and 35 move us forward from the darkness and the cold to the rustle of spring and the realisation of our dreams

There are other more 'open-ended' interpretations. The world as it is (Isaiah 34) and the world as God intended it (Isaiah 35). Where we are and where God wants us. How to share in the experiences of the people described in chapter 34. Where to find them, and how to work out what it means to 'speak to their heart' (40.2, NJB) and begin to build a highway to a renewed world.

But in a day when there is so much emphasis on ecology and the environment, one possibility is to take the desert literally and see whether the two chapters, taken together, might enrich the story of Christmas and our understanding of the incarnation.

Genesis 1–11 portrays a God concerned with land, with earthiness, with the natural world as well as the human. Both accounts of creation (Genesis 1.1 to 2.4a and 2.4b-25) focus on the physical world as much as on humanity. Both emphases persist throughout the biblical narrative, out of which comes the concept of a totally new creation and, especially in the later writings, the notion of Wisdom existing before the creation of the world. New Testament writers inherited these ideas to present Christ as the one to inaugurate the new creation of the universe as well as humanity (for example, Romans 8.19–21, 2 Corinthians 5.17 and Hebrews 1.2–3).

dreams of Israel (the 'haves') and opening the door to the Gentiles (the 'have-nots'). This can now be celebrated. This is where the highway we have to build must lead us.

Wholeness is about belonging. Matthew 1.1–16 may not be the most scintillating passage to be read in church. Its historical accuracy may be questionable, and perish the thought that anyone should preach on it, but it is a valuable resource.

It puts this baby in a wider setting, shows where he came from and where he belongs. By rooting him firmly in the Jewish tradition, the genealogy lays claim to Jewish loyalty and demonstrates that this new 'Christianity' – which took its rise from his arrival – was not a new faith, or a different faith, but one rooted in the faith 'once for all delivered to the saints'.

To the Jews it ensures that the treasures of the old established community are not usurped by a new movement. To the Christians it relates the newly-emerging and uncertain Christian groupings to the wider and earlier Jewish community. Christmas is a time to celebrate togetherness in a community where individuals derive their distinction less from their individuality and more from their lineage and linkages. Everyone belongs to him, and he belongs to everyone.

Wholeness is about tension

But the old ties of kinship are only part of the story. They are important but not over-riding. Wholeness is also about equality. There are others who have to be brought in and recognised as equals. Officers must learn to wait at table, and owners, managers, supervisors and humble workers must meet and greet on the same level and in the same way, even if only for a season. The story only comes alive when everybody 'belongs' and nobody is excluded and, where it doesn't exist, the story requires us to create it.

And therein lies the rub. Wholeness is about tension. Christmas always and inevitably highlights the tension between those with whom we can celebrate easily and happily and those we find difficult, between 'settling down with your own' and maintaining an awareness of the others.

It surfaces in the tension between Jesus and his family on the one hand and Jesus with his 'new family' of disciples (and perhaps also the women) on the other (Luke 2.48–50). The seeds of growing apart are being sown; somebody needs to be alert to them, focus on them and seek to bring healing. Jesus, with his single-mindedness, has hurt his family, unwittingly no doubt. They, on the other hand, show a lack of awareness and understanding. But what is the value of accepting the sinner and the rejected if the price is to reject the already accepted?

It is the tension between those who belong and those who feel as if they do not belong: some, like the Jews, who feel they have been taken over by the 'new brigade' and no longer count; others, like the Gentiles, who feel they lack the right labels and qualifications; and many in between, like Paul, who have tried to build bridges and now feel as if they don't belong either. And the way we celebrate will not only reflect how much wholeness already exists but also determine how much richer it becomes in the future.

Conclusion

The whole Bible is about Christmas

'Christmas' does not feature in the Bible because the whole Bible is about Christmas: the creation, re-creation and renewal of the whole world for all God's creatures and made possible only through our co-operation with him.

Perhaps that was what Paul meant when he said of the Spirit, that 'in everything, as we know, he co-operates for good with those who love God and are called according to his purpose' (Romans 8.28, REB).

'A book full of stories...'

A prayer for Bible Sunday, the Second Sunday of Advent

God of all our words and wonderings,
our choices and rejections,
our beginnings and endings,
help us to value rightly
that great collection
of human dreams and visions
we call the Bible.

***We celebrate the wonder of many stories
and the joy of the whole story.***

Give us imagination
  that we may read with open minds;
  find life in words;
  become part of the story.

***We celebrate the wonder of many stories
and the joy of the whole story.***

Give us insight
  that we may discern what is good;
  discover what is hidden;
  dance to life's rhythm
  in poetry and song.

***We celebrate the wonder of many stories
and the joy of the whole story.***

Give us understanding
  that the Bible, gifted from the past,
  with power still to move and change,
  may be for us the way
  not the end of our dreaming;
  that justice, joy and outspoken love
  may be the hope we release
  from ancient stories
  into today's world.

***We celebrate the wonder of many stories
and the joy of the whole story.***

Joy Mead

Bethlehem lies dreaming

Bright moon, scattered stars; so solitary is creation. The universe which God has created is especially silent on this night. It waits with bated breath for the Lord of Creation to return. The universe belongs to God, it is his home.

Silence reigns supreme. The flowers of the field sway gently in the moonlight. This night, the vast earth awaits the homecoming of our Creator God. The vast earth and open fields belong to God, they are his home.

Bethlehem lies dreaming. In his gentle mother's arms, the babe sleeps peacefully this night. The City of David awaits the homecoming of David's descendant. The town of Bethlehem belongs to him, it is his home.

My bones, my flesh, my blood, my lungs and my heart, were all made by his hand. This night, my heart is at peace, awaiting my Creator's return. My heart belongs to him, it is his home.

Wang Weifan
From *Lilies of the Field*, Foundation for Theological Education in South East Asia

West Africa to work in conditions of great cruelty and hardship in the sugar plantations. It speaks of the huge debt imposed on Haiti when she gained independence from France. It speaks of the poverty resulting from the loans made to the corrupt Duvalier regimes. Although the poor never benefited from these loans, they are the ones paying the price today. Debt and the corruption engendered by dire poverty are woven together into Haiti's tragic history.

In the Haiti Jubilee 2000 office in Port au Prince we were told, 'Haiti's debt is unjust and immoral.' Eddy Lacoste and his colleagues in the office were committed to the debt cancellation campaign not just for the people of Haiti but for all highly indebted poor countries. They had collected 100 000 signatures for the Jubilee 2000 petition and were raising awareness through schools and churches. Eddy was determined that debt would not continue for ever to be a part of Haiti's story, that the rod of their oppressors should at last be broken. 'We want debt remission and transparency. Debt cancellation is linked to a new state we want to create.' Eddy showed us the poster which had been designed by the Episcopal Justice and Peace Commission. The image of the cross symbolised debt, the arm of the cross the burden of debt crushing the backs of the poor.

Out of their history and in the midst of their present reality, the people look to God for a sign that there is some better prospect for their country

Out of their history and in the midst of their present reality, the people look to God for a sign that there is some better prospect for their country. There are few cars on the dirt-track country roads of Haiti, but there are buses. Every bus is painted in wonderful bright, psychedelic patterns and festooned with decorations and ribbons. The roof is piled high with baskets of fruit and vegetables and people wedged between. Inside the bus there is music, chatter and laughter with people happily offering seats on their knees to those standing for long distances. The city buses are called 'Tap taps' because when you want to get off you bang on the side! Old and broken down as they are, the buses witness vividly to the hope of the people, each one painted with slogans which read 'L'amour de Dieu' or 'Le Seigneur est bon', boldly proclaiming the coming of the Kingdom. The principal sign of hope offered by the prophet Isaiah is the future contained in the birth of the child: 'a son given to us'. Of him the prophet said: he is to be a 'Wonderful Counsellor, Mighty God, Everlasting Father, Prince of Peace' and 'his authority shall grow continually and there shall be endless peace' (Isaiah 9.1–7).

Where is the future saviour of Haiti to be born?

He will not come from within the tiny number of elite families who seek to control the life of the people for their own benefit. David, the hope of Israel, was found among the poverty and insignificance of the keepers of sheep. The future ruler of Haiti will come from the poverty of one of the remote village communities, or from the squalor of the shanty towns of Port au Prince.

The shanty towns sprawl up the surrounding hillsides. Narrow alleys link the tightly packed shacks, but you have to walk with care as these alleys also serve as open drains. Each shack is built of concrete blocks with a roof of corrugated iron to keep out the sun and rain. There are no windows; it has a mud floor and is about eight feet square. Here whole families live with no running water, sanitation or even basic furniture. When it is time to go to sleep you simply put a few clothes down on the floor and lie down. But there are worse places than the shanty town on the hillside. Below, even more unhealthy but cheaper, is the City L'éternel stretching right down to the water's edge. So unsuitable for housing is this land that there was nothing there before 1989. Then a group of squatters began to occupy the land because they had nowhere else to go.

Haiti's saviour will not come from within the tiny number of elite families who seek to control the life of the people

In these places, whether town or country, basic health care is offered by too few clinics, and many children do not survive. But one child will survive who will be their saviour. This is their advent hope.

Daring to dream

The prophet describes his dreams of the coming Kingdom in poetic language: 'the wolf shall live with the lamb and the leopard shall lie down with the kid' (Isaiah 11.1–9). His dream is for a reversal of this world's order, its expectations and its values. Much of the hope still alive among the Haitian people is found expressed in music and art and metal work. On the wall of our living room is a mythical bird perched in a flowering tree, finely crafted from the metal of an oil drum. The metal worker, whom we visited in his small workshop, has taken something old and discarded, and lovingly moulded it into something new and beautiful. Old oil drums are transformed into vivid colourful creations. This is a different symbolism from that of 8th century BC Israel, but it serves the same purpose – a sign of hope amidst the hopelessness of human fear, poverty and misery.

Some of the hopes and fears of Haitian people are expressed in voodoo. We were taken to a small voodoo temple, down a dark back alley. For us, the atmosphere inside felt sinister and forbidding. The priest was friendly to us, trying hard to present his voodoo faith in ways which might be acceptable to Christians. He talked about overcoming the powers of evil, but left us with the impression that he was more concerned with appeasing the powers of evil than confronting them. He also believed very strongly in his own power over people. There is no doubt that voodoo has helped an abused people discover, retain and express their African identity. But our visit left us sure that there is no sustaining hope to be found in the fear of those who believe in the power of the voodoo priest. The real source of hope and dreams lies elsewhere.

The 'dare to dream' is rightly often rooted in the past. Isaiah was able to dream about the future only by drawing on the memories of the rule of David, generations before. In the central public square in Port au Prince, there is a statue of Toussaint Louverture. He is revered as the leader who transformed groups of *Maroons* (escaped slaves) into a seasoned and disciplined army of liberation. Toussaint Louverture dared to dream, to dream of liberty for his people. But he paid the price; eventually he was betrayed and died in a French gaol.

There is a statue also of Jean-Jacques Dessalines, an illiterate former slave whose back bore the scars of lashings administered by his owners. Dessalines became the founder of the independent republic of Haiti and is remembered each year with a national holiday on 17 October, the date of his death in 1806. It is the memory of these people's lives which provides hope for the future. For the people of Haiti, these collective memories are a source of cohesion, identity and a belief in themselves. 'If once we produced a leader like that,' they say in much the same way as David was remembered, 'then one day we shall produce another. And this one too will lead us out of slavery into a better future. He will be our saviour.'

Isaiah spoke of an ideal figure who will rule in righteousness and establish justice. There is a strong element of longing throughout Isaiah: if only there were such a king who would reign in righteousness, then the princes will rule in justice. In Haiti, this same 'if only' dream

Isaiah spoke of an ideal figure who will rule in righteousness and establish justice

is sustained not only by the lives of these past leaders but also by people today who already live by the values of the Kingdom.

Elicoeur Beaubrun lives in Mare Rouge, a small town in the remote North-west of Haiti. He is a community health worker, unpaid because the clinic has no money to employ even his trained labour. Elicoeur visits people in their homes, takes part in the health education programme using local radio, gives vaccinations and advice on family planning. He receives no income, but his family of four children live off the small piece of land which he farms, and on what his wife sells in the market place. When he was 14, he decided to dedicate his life to serving the community in which he lives. He is a respected man in that community and a sacristan in his local church. There, in 1999, he heard about the Jubilee 2000 campaign. Immediately, he saw that this was something he could do and he set about collecting signatures for the petitions asking for debt remission. He wanted debt remission not just for his own country but for the oppressed poor throughout the world.

A commitment to justice and service is not an unrealistic ideal

The head of the clinic at Mare Rouge is Dr Kenson Alsena. His small clinic serves a community of 20 000 people. The clinic has very limited access to the one ambulance which services a region of 200 000 people. Dr Kenson leads a small team of paid health workers and a larger team of health workers and community mid-wives who, like Elicoeur, work without pay for the love of their community. Together, they are slowly building a community of more healthy people, with basic medical care, cement latrines, water and food. Their approach is holistic, for they know that 'empty sacks cannot stand up'.

It is these people – and many others like them – who keep alive the hope of the coming of the Kingdom. Their manner of life shows that a commitment to justice and service is not an unrealistic ideal. It is a way in which the advent hope of the coming of Christ in their time is expressed. They are the ones who 'listen with the ears' and 'look with the eyes' of the Kingdom, to use Isaiah's imagery. Their vision is expressed in simple but dedicated practical living. It is a light in the darkness which enables others to keep on believing in the coming Kingdom.

The desert shall rejoice

Isaiah's vision was not confined to the ordering of human affairs – justice for the poor and peace between people.

His vision included the transformation of nature, seen for example in his poetic language of wolf and lamb, leopard and kid, calf and lion, cow and bear, lion and ox (Isaiah 11.1–9). The prophet also uses vivid imagery to express his vision for the renewal of the natural order:

> **The wilderness and the dry land shall be glad,**
> **the desert shall rejoice and blossom;**
> **like the crocus it shall blossom abundantly**
> **and rejoice with joy and singing.**
>
> (Isaiah 35.1)

These powerful images relate directly to Haiti's expectation of the coming of the Kingdom. Much of the Haitian countryside has been destroyed. Hillsides are left bare: trees have been cut down to make charcoal, the only source of fuel for cooking. On the north-west coast of Haiti, at the very place where Christopher Columbus – the man who is remembered in Haiti for the murder of the indigenous Indians — landed, there is an idyllic and deserted beach, a holiday brochure scene to tempt the non-existent tourist. Bathing in the clean warm waters of this beach, you are surrounded by the bare and desolate hillsides, once rich with forest. A few hundred yards away in the harbour, the boats are laden with thousands of sacks of charcoal, destined for the population of Port au Prince. In many places in rural Haiti, reafforestation schemes are the source of hope for the future, so that soil may be retained and the rainfall feed rather than destroy the crops. Much of this replanting, encouraged by rural projects supported by the church in partnership with Christian Aid, is of mango trees, a favourite tree because it provides fruit as well as reafforestation.

In many places in rural Haiti, reafforestation schemes are the source of hope for the future

Isaiah's vision of the future Kingdom also speaks of 'a hiding place from the wind, a covert from the tempest' (Isaiah 32.2). In Haiti, those who live in the shanty towns which make up most of Port au Prince have little or no shelter from torrential rain which sweeps down the hillsides, destroying all before it and undermining the foundations of the rough human shelters. As elsewhere in the Caribbean, hurricanes bring extensive damage to the country, further destroying what is left of the forests so essential for the fertility of the land. It is always the poor who suffer most from natural disaster, for usually they have no protection. Isaiah looks for a future society where the ordinary people are able to find some protection, some 'shelter from the storm'. The dream of the people of Haiti is for a just and caring government which will seek to provide 'a hiding place from the wind'.

'However bad today is, tomorrow may be better'

This is a common saying in Haiti. In part it expresses a mood of resignation; but in part it also expresses a note of hope. The hope is not just that surely things cannot get much worse. It is a much more positive hope, springing from the heart of a remarkably resilient people, that one day things will be better. There will be a tomorrow.

Isaiah speaks of a new highway for his people. This new highway is called 'the Holy Way' (Isaiah 35.8). It is the road on which the people will walk with God on a new exodus journey into a new promised land. The first exodus journey was a geographical one through the forty years of wilderness. But it was also an inner journey, a spiritual pilgrimage, a time of learning, moulding and growing in understanding of what it meant to be God's people. It was a time of becoming what God willed and dreamed and hoped for them. Some of the people of Haiti see their way ahead as a physical journey, escaping across the Caribbean Sea to the United States, a land of plenty, flowing with milk and honey. But most of the Haitian people know that their way ahead does not lie in such escape. This would be 'to put their trust in foreign powers', the very thing that the prophet Isaiah urges the king not to do.

There will be a tomorrow

Yet for many Haitians who live in a poverty-stricken countryside there is a desire to make a geographical move, a move from countryside to city. This is an expression of hope. The rural life offers little prospect and sometimes barely enough food. The land is bare, the topsoil washed away, and the crops have failed again. Like people living on poor land throughout the world, they hear that life is better in the city. So off they go, with their few possessions on the roof of the bus, if they are lucky. Otherwise they trudge to Port au Prince, their dream capital city, their hope of a new Jerusalem. There they find a new sort of poverty: an acute shortage of space on which to build a shelter, an unpayable rent for a small one-roomed house which comes without water or sanitation. Here they are trapped, living off almost nothing, supported often by non-government aid agencies and a little haggling, selling on the streets. Their road has been a 'nowhere else to go' journey and it is not the highway to a new future. For the vast majority who walk this route, it is a dead-end journey to misery. Even here, the spirit is not quenched, and hope is kept alive that 'tomorrow may be better'.

There are other highways to be sought and walked, and again Isaiah provides an evocative image. For one of the ways in which Isaiah pictures the way ahead is to describe it as a time when the dumb will speak (Isaiah 32.4). He is speaking about the powerless having a say in their own future. In Haiti, a principal way ahead for the poor is to learn to read and write, a process which empowers those who are otherwise always reliant on others and unable to move forward themselves. Literacy is a powerful tool, denied to the majority of the people where over 50% of the adult population is illiterate.

Visiting the South-west of Haiti, we met with groups of people who had begun to discover the difference it made when the dumb were able to speak. One middle-aged man spoke of the confidence he now had to go into the nearest small town on his own. He was able to read the sign on the bus, see the names of the shops, buy the goods that he needed, all because he was now able to read. A woman proud to have her two children at school found that now she could read their school reports for herself. 'The children used to tell me how well they had done and how pleased the teacher was with them,' she told us. 'Now,' she said with a little laugh, 'they come home at the end of term and try to hide their reports because they know that I can read them for myself!' Behind these stories there is a discovery of a new dignity. The powerless are able to read and write, and therefore to speak. Education is one of the marks of the way forward, one of the signposts on the new highway to a better future.

Education is one of the marks of the way forward, one of the signposts on the new highway to a better future

The sound of your laughter

It is lovely to read in Luke's Gospel about Mary's visit to her cousin Elizabeth. 'When Elizabeth heard Mary's greeting, the child leapt in her womb.' These two women, one old, one young, but both pregnant for the first time, have already shown their trust in God. Such trust undoubtedly enables the two of them to be free to enjoy one another's company, offering companionship and support to each other. They are clearly thrilled to be together and Mary remains with Elizabeth for three months.

Companionship and support are sometimes all that women have to offer each other. But these things can be invaluable, and the signs of hope in many of the world's poorest communities are often more clearly seen in the women.

In the west of Haiti, near the small town of Petit Goave, a group had formed the Women's Community Bank. 'We started the scheme because we are all poor. We sat under the mango tree to put our heads together,' said Antoinette. Sylvie explained, 'You sign up to be a member, go to meetings and then qualify for a loan.' Another woman added, 'I have set up a little business selling washing basins, knives, forks and spoons. Now I have some money to spend on the children, I can send them to school. If they are ill, I can pay for health care.'

Another of the women talked about the difference her small business had made in her relationship with her husband. She wasn't dependent on him now, she explained, and she had a little money in her pocket. So her husband had started calling her 'dear' and 'love'! We all laughed.

Companionship and support are sometimes all that women have to offer each other

The women meet every week under the mango tree. They talk about how to manage their business better, how to work well together as a group, and they sing and pray together. 'If you can't pay back your loan, others will help you,' they said.

We will never forget another woman we met in Port au Prince. Her poster is on the wall of our study and her name is Rosanne Auguste. The poster advertises Rosanne's music and there are several pictures of her singing, recording, laughing. By day, Rosanne runs a clinic in the shanty towns of Port au Prince, providing essential health care services to the thousands of people who live in the over-crowded, insanitary conditions. In the evenings, Rosanne sings.

One night, on a roof top in Port au Prince, under a star-lit Caribbean sky, we danced to the music of a Haitian street band playing three string guitars, maracas and drums. And then, quietly, with a single guitarist as accompaniment, we gathered round as Rosanne sang. She sang, in her native Creole, of the history and struggles of her people.

Pour faire avancer la barque
Ainsi, mon amour,
Sur ton rire, viendra la frénésie du monde.
We must sail forward into the future
And then, my love, from the sound of your
laughter
will come the energy to save the world.

In this haunting melody is expressed the advent hope of Haiti.

*'...from the
sound of
laughter will
come the
energy to save
the world'*

A new road

Lord,
We know that the present is not heaven.
In so many ways, our world is not at all like heaven.
But we also know a little of your dreams.
We have seen in the words of the prophets
and in the lives of your followers,
a glimpse of your hopes for all creation.
We dare to look with hope to the future:
good news for the poor,
release for the oppressed.

Lord,
In Jesus, you too knew what it is like to feel
abandoned.
When we feel cut off, you share that experience
with us.
Open our eyes that we may see your presence
in the quiet and unspectacular lives
of those who simply seek to do what they can,
and in so doing become signs of your living
presence.
Let us watch for your coming.
Let us be faithful to the One who has come,
is here and has pledged to come,
again and again.

Lord,
Through the prophets and your servant John the
Baptist,
you prepared a new road and invited us to travel
on it
with each other and with you.
It is the road of justice for all,
of caring for each other,
of living together as community.
Teach us to value your way and not our own.
Help us to seek justice and peace for others
and not just for ourselves and our friends.
Enable us to work for change in your world
by accepting your power to bring change in our
own lives.
May we work with you to clear a new road ahead,
so that your justice may find expression
throughout your world. Amen

Barbara and David Calvert

cigarettes or matches in the streets, washing cars or simply begging.

Unfortunately the presence of drug traffickers in our communities has brought problems. It is easy for them to hide and run their business in such an environment. Many times the police come and treat us all as if we were bandits. But the major problem is that many of our children and teenagers are responding positively to the proposals of traffickers who offer positions in their business, sometimes for a large amount of money in comparison with what they would earn from honest work. The majority of those involved in the drug traffic in Brazilian big cities are between ten and twenty-five years of age.

For most people there is no choice – many work hard in the hope that their children will escape this situation and have a better life. We know that life is getting hard for the poor but we also know that if we help each other our situation will improve. We believe that real change will only come about through the actions of poor people themselves.

Homeless people speak...

There are hundreds of us in Rio. Many of us live in the streets because we have come from the countryside where life was even worse. As we do not have an address it is difficult to find work and often there is not enough money to feed the family or have a house.

Others of our group have had somewhere to live before. They were paying rent to live in poor houses but they had a home. But with today's high unemployment rate, they have lost their jobs or sometimes the salary becomes so small – they have to negotiate to continue working – that they cannot afford to pay their rent. They are evicted from their homes and have nowhere to go.

Most distressing of all is the plight of our children and teenagers. Their main objective is to survive so they earn money by shining shoes, washing cars, or selling sweets or newspapers. But they also beg, pick pockets, steal, mug or search litter bins. Their need often leads to glue-sniffing, drug or alcohol addiction and prostitution with the danger of getting AIDS. Such children are often exploited by adults and subjected to horrendous violence at the hands of the police, adults or death squads.

So, we are here living on the streets. It is a life that nobody wants. We cannot take a bath, sleep in a bed or cook our food. We suffer when it rains and the weather is cold. Many people are afraid of us, thinking that we will do something

Real change will only come about through the actions of poor people themselves

bad to them, and the police come many times to drive us away. But what can we do? Where can we go? The situation seems to get worse because every day new people come to live on the streets.

Rio workers speak...

We are the millions of people of Rio who work for commerce, banks, financial companies, middle-class houses, private enterprises, schools, governmental and multinational companies.

The majority of us have to live on the edge of Rio because it is cheaper to buy a house or to pay rent in those areas. Because of this, every morning we have to leave our house at 5.30am to be at work by 8.00am and we rarely get home before 8.00pm. Sometimes, when we are forced to work overtime, it is even later. We do not like doing overtime because our day is already too long, but we have no choice. There is the risk of being fired if we object. And we know there are plenty of other people ready to replace us, although what companies pay us is a 'whipping wage'...

We will keep up our struggle, otherwise how can we survive?

We hardly have any leisure time with our families as we struggle to pay our bills and buy food. Sometimes, to supplement our income, we need to find other jobs to work in the evening or at weekends, or to work in the so-called 'informal economy' (selling things in the streets, for example). Wives have to work as housemaids or washerwomen. Children also work to help but we want our children in school.

Trade unions have struggled a lot. Sometimes we get the improvements we ask for but sometimes not. Our demands disturb the investments of business people and the Parliament has voted in different projects to reduce our historical rights. We will keep up our struggle, otherwise how can we survive?

Judging...

The image on postcards or in tourist guide books of the Redeemer Christ on the top of a mountain in Rio has attracted millions of visitors. Christ's arms are open above the city and over all those who visit the mountain... It is a beautiful symbol but it is also a provocative image. This mountain is located in the south zone of Rio, the rich part of the city, facing the sea. Is Christ really standing there? Where is Christ in Rio?

The birth of Jesus Christ, as recorded in the first two chapters of Luke's Gospel, gives us clues to answer these questions. Luke shares with us the truth that through the birth of that child the Lord God was challenging his people to understand his will and promises. What does Luke say?

God chooses a woman

Women suffered serious discrimination in the Jewish society of that time. By choosing to send the Saviour through the womb of a woman, having to depend on her care and attention to survive, God reminds us of the value he puts on women and their struggle for a place in society. On the other hand, God gave Mary a difficult task: she was going to be pregnant before her marriage to her fiancé Joseph. If an ordinary woman was discriminated against and disregarded at that time, what about a woman being pregnant before getting married? What a hard situation to face for the sake of a promise! Matthew writes that Joseph, knowing that Mary was pregnant, did not want to disgrace her publicly and made plans to break the engagement privately (Matthew 1.18–19). Despite all these adversities, however, the angel says to Mary: 'Nothing will be impossible with God' (Luke 1.37). Perhaps it was fear of public disgrace led by those who could not understand the purpose of God, as Joseph could, that made Mary get ready and hurry off to Elizabeth's house, a 'visit' that lasted three months (1.39–56).

God reminds us of the value he puts on women and their struggle for a place in society

Jesus is born among the poor

In her meeting with her cousin Elizabeth, who was six months pregnant with John the Baptist, Mary finally understood the meaning of her task to give birth to the Saviour of the world. Elizabeth experienced a revelation as Mary entered the house and so helped her to understand that the child in her womb was blessed by God and so was Mary for daring to believe what was happening to her (1.39–45). The song of praise which follows (Luke 1.46–55) expresses her conviction that she was chosen, a poor, young, simple and single woman. The Lord intended to scatter the proud with all their plans, to bring down mighty kings from their thrones and lift up the lowly. He would fill the hungry with good things, sending the rich away with empty hands. The key word of Mary's praise is *mercy*.

The Lord God is the God of the poor and humble, of the discriminated and excluded. That was the revelation that had its climax in Jesus' birth in poverty: there was no room for them anywhere – only a poor and dirty stable. And the first people to witness the birth of the Saviour were poor, simple shepherds of the fields (2.1–20). Jesus' ministry confirmed Mary's song of praise showed his mercy and love when walking alongside the ill, the children, the women, the peasants, the fishermen, all those excluded from citizenship and religion.

Mary was very brave to take up this challenge to be the mother of God's Son. Not only did she face public disgrace, she and her family had to flee from the power of Herod – the proud and mighty who would be brought down from his throne, the rich who would be sent away with empty hands, and who was upset by the new order Jesus was going to establish (Matthew 2.1–6). Mary and her husband Joseph had to escape to the land of Egypt, to guarantee Jesus' survival, for Herod, King of Judea, furious at the news of Jesus' birth, ordered the massacre of all boys who were two years old and younger (Matthew 2.16–18). It was a hard time for all those families.

It was no different from the hard life of *favela* dwellers, homeless people and workers in Rio. As in the past, the powers of the present time do not want change, new perspectives, the new order that could be established by the Kingdom of God. This is why they enact a modern version in the streets of Rio of the killing ordered by King Herod. Herod is present in the death squads who kill the children who live in the streets, killing the possibility of change, of a new perspective...

Herod is present in the death squads who kill the children who live in the streets, killing the possibility of change

The story of Jesus' birth lives on in every time and place: in Rio de Janeiro and in every part of the world. In Rio, however, one barrier has always been the meaning given to Christmas. The denial of our roots and culture, masked by the ideal of 'globalisation', and a total surrender to the lifestyle of the rich world, has brought to our relaxed hot, green and rainy Christmas time the 'white' scenery of modern shopping centres that dictate who is able to take part and who is not. They marginalise the image of Jesus to a distant manger or to the top of a mountain.

Learning from Jesus and recovering Mary's revelation, we cannot believe that the Redeemer Christ stands on the mountain, above all, distant... Jesus Christ is born again, every day, in the midst of street families who, like his family, find no room anywhere. Jesus is walking every day in the narrow paths of the *favelas*, alongside the people who go out into the streets to earn some money and survive. Yes, he is there! Jesus Christ is present in the homes of workers, in the outskirts, like Nazareth, where he was brought up. Every day, Jesus is sharing the struggles and hopes of the people who live in a wonderful city but who do not have the time or means to enjoy its beauties. But they do find strength to go ahead and enjoy the simple fact of being alive.

Acting...

Mary was a simple, poor young woman who received a serious and difficult task. She accepted and was blessed with the full understanding of the meaning of her task: to bring to the world the One who would lift up the lowly and the excluded. Mary faced barriers imposed by the imperialist, patriarchal and sexist society of her time and played her role.

There are many occasions in churches in Rio when people allow Jesus to be born in their lives: they experience personal change and they commit themselves to change some of the political and social structures which impoverish their families and communities. God also acts outside the church and calls people to act in his name, to plant the seeds of the Kingdom.

Let us share some stories of church people who are 'Mary' today... Maybe Laura is...

Laura's story:

'I am thirty-five years old and have four children. I live in the *Baixada Fluminense* (an area in the outskirts of Rio) and my life, like the lives of the others who dwell here, is very hard.

'My husband works in the chemical industry. We do not have our own house and have to rent one. I cannot take a job because I have to look after my children. But as my husband's salary is too small to support the family, I do some work to help to pay our expenses, especially our rent. I know how to sew, so I can work at home making or repairing clothes. I also prepare cakes for birthdays and wedding parties.

'But the best part of my life is to belong to the church. I have been a member for more than ten years and it is very good for me because we gather together as a community. Everybody has problems but we worship together and learn how God looks after us and gives us strength.

'Our church has ninety members and is very lively. Every Sunday morning we meet for teaching in Sunday School

Mary faced barriers imposed by the imperialist, patriarchal and sexist society of her time

and in the evening we gather together for worship. In Sunday School, where I am in one of the classes for people of my age, we talk a lot and discover how the Bible helps us to understand our life with God today and how God is acting and speaking to us.

'I have learnt that when we are together we find strength to struggle for a better life in the area where we live and in our country. God wants our happiness and we have a job to do as God's children, joining groups in our community who struggle for what we need: health, education, houses, clean water, paved streets, a better life for children who live in the streets. Our church opens its doors to receive people from the community to have debates about our needs and what we can do together. It is a great testimony!

'I also take part in the Decoration and Parties Ministry. I am the leader! Everyone in the church is asked to offer what gifts and service they can to God and the community. We decorate the church every Sunday and prepare for special events and parties. At Christmas we decorate a pine tree with coloured ornaments and prepare a big table to be shared by all people who come.'

Monica's story...

'I am twelve years old. I do not live with my family because it is very poor and big – I have nine brothers and sisters and it is not possible for my parents to look after all of us. So we live with different families who give us shelter, food, school and clothes, and we help them with the housework.

'It was good for me that the family that looks after me goes to church. There I can take part in a community to study the Bible, sing and have friends. Many of my friends live as I do.

'Because of my age, I am not sure if I am a child or a teenager. But I can say that we have lots of children and young people in our church. We enjoy helping the church's work, doing everything that we can: sometimes we help to prepare the church hall for worship; sometimes we go with the minister to visit sick people; sometimes we have fund-raising activities for church projects.

'It is good because we learn that children and young people are important to the life of the community and that we are needed and valued by the church now. Because of this, all of us try to discover what our gifts are and put them to God's service.'

When we are together we find strength to struggle for a better life in the area where we live and in our country

Can a man play Mary's role?
What about Mario...?

'Like almost everybody who lives in the *Baixada Fluminense*, my family came from the countryside to try to make a better life in a big city. I am sixty-seven years old and retired but as the pension that I receive from the government is very, very small, I have to work to increase my income to maintain my family. I work as a night-caretaker in a factory. Many retired people in Brazil do the same. During the day I like to do other things: to build and repair houses and work as a carpenter.

'I have been a Christian since I was young, in my small town in the countryside, and the church is part of my life. I very much like teaching a class for adults in Sunday School, and so I am part of the Christian Education Ministry. I also enjoy handicrafts, and when I am at home I make wooden toys and other things. Then I organise quizzes with children and teenagers, and the winners receive the toys I make. And the adults like to play as well...

'I like to give my free time to the church and help in everything I can. I like to take part in prayer meetings arranged by the women's organisation. Every week we go to different homes to reflect together on the Bible and share our lives (our problems and good moments) and we pray together. It gives us strength to face our daily life. We do not feel that we are alone but that we are part of a community of brothers and sisters.

'I work all night on Saturday. Everyone says that I ought to go home to rest but I go straight to the church, hiding my bicycle, because, as I said, the church is so much a part of my life.'

Praying gives us strength to face our daily life

Today, in Rio de Janeiro and in all parts of the world that face the same contradiction between a life of beauty and wonder and a life of poverty and suffering, the Lord God is calling people to be the bearers of his mercy and love. He calls them to give birth to Jesus Christ in people's hearts and renew their hope to live and change the world that continues pushing down the poor and humble and excluding the sick, the disabled, the children, the women, the labourers... Let us, like Mary, remove the barriers to our task, and help Jesus to be born again and again as the Saviour of the world.

I put my life in your hands

Dear Lord,
I praise you for your mercy and love,
as did your daughter Mary in the past,
because your name is holy;
from one generation to another,
you show mercy to those who honour you.
You have stretched out your mighty arm
and scattered the proud with all their plans.
You have brought down mighty governors
from their cabinets,
and lifted up the lowly.
You have filled the hungry with good things,
and sent the rich away with empty hands.
You have kept the promise you made to our
ancestors,
and have come to the help of your people.
You have remembered to show mercy to Abraham
and to all your servants for ever.

I put my life in your hands, O Lord,
to be your instrument and bear your will
through the name of Jesus Christ,
the Child born among the poor.
Help me to overcome all barriers
that may prevent me from serving you,
and to make Christmas a time of repentance,
mercy and conversion.
In your name I pray. Amen

Magali do Nascimento Cunha

The space between...

God of fragile new life,
take us to the space
between Annunciation and Magnificat
where hope is all and words come
tumbling out.
Open our eyes, our hearts, our minds
to the excitement of ordinary meetings
and everyday happenings;
to the leaping of babies
and the conversations of home.
Help us, like Mary and Elizabeth,
to join hands
in commitment, companionship
and affirmation
as the Spirit prompts us
to set out with joy
into wide and unknown futures.

Joy Mead

OLord almighty who has mysteriously revealed to the sages of old your ineffable presence in the depth of the heart, grant to us and also to those of our brothers and sisters who follow in their footsteps that being led by your holy Spirit in this inward search we may discover therein the light incorruptible, your divine Son, Jesus Christ our Lord, for ever and ever. Amen

The Holy Eucharist: Forms of Worship, Jyotiniketan Ashram, North India and Jerusalem

4
Discovering Christ in rural India

Israel Selvanayagam

Micah 5.2
Luke 2.1–20
Matthew 2.1–23
Philippians 2.5–11

In the midst of darkness and dirt, the child Jesus shines forth and calls all people to bow down before him and co-operate with him to create a new world.

Christmas in Parakkanvilai

My home village is Parakkanvilai, a hamlet on the southern tip of India, and less than a mile from the shores of the Indian Ocean. The people there have a slogan: 'When Jesus the Lord is born, we have meat curry.' Meat is a rarity for them. Fish, rice and tapioca are their staple diet; the majority are very poor. Nearly half of the 6 000 villagers are illiterate and live below the poverty line.

For the majority of people in rural India, the next mealtime hangs on chance. It depends on the availability of work and the prompt payment of wages for the breadwinner (usually the man of the family). Half of the population in Parakkanvilai are Christians, and most are members of the local church which belongs to the Church of South India. In the last century, there was a mass conversion to Christianity in that area in the wake of a riot called 'the upper cloth movement'. Some of them, encouraged by missionaries, dared to wear upper garments in public places to defy an age-long rule imposed by high caste Hindus. Many who became Christians were persecuted.

'When Jesus the Lord is born, we have meat curry'

Christmas always brings new life to Parakkanvilai. Visiting homes and carol singing starts on Advent Sunday and ends on the day before Christmas Eve. When I lived there, each day from 6.30 in the evening until midnight, a group of young men went around to the homes with a drum and other rhythmic instruments, singing carols. Sometimes we divided the group into two to cover different areas and to finish earlier. A petromax light (push lamp) shone, breaking up the darkness of all the nooks and crannies. In those days there was no electricity and even today only a few homes are supplied with the minimum of light. We sang standing in the courtyard of each house and sometimes the group was invited in for refreshments, and a lay church worker said a word of prayer. Sometimes we sang at homes of non-CSI members, including Catholics and even Hindus. There was no end of humour! Today Hindus also do something similar, going around with devotional chants, and at times the groups bump into each other with smiles and jokes!

This tradition is still alive in the villages, though with fewer participants as more young people go away to find work. And it does more than celebrate Christmas: it calls to mind a bitter experience in the past and is an affirmation of hope. A few generations ago, with great suddenness, a terrible plague of cholera took many lives, and no medical help was available. It was left to a group of brave men to bury the dead, one after another. People did not dare to come out of their houses in the evening and so, to reassure them, members of the local church went around with a push lamp, beating drums and singing songs of comfort and encouragement. That is why, even today, songs other than carols are included in the Advent carol singing. The main purpose is to be present, alongside the people, giving them hope. Throughout Advent, the birth of Jesus is symbolised by the shining of light, the sound of the drum and the renewal of life.

Although there is a worship service on Christmas morning at 5.00am, the main service is on Christmas Eve, lasting for five hours and finishing around midnight. Children take part with great enthusiasm, wearing new clothes, the only guaranteed gifts of the year from their parents. They contribute songs, dialogues, sketches and recitations of verses from the Bible. They never tire of repeating the themes of light and glory and, as they bend down and touch the earth with its dirt and pollution, they re-enact the way that God demonstrated his supreme love in the birth of Jesus by coming down to us, and the renewal of life he offers through giving and forgiving. Children also frequently expose the irresponsible behaviour of men who get drunk at Christmas and beat their wives and children, making Christmas a day of fear, bitterness, tears. Poor widows are presented with saris in this service and children receive prizes and gifts.

The birth of Jesus is symbolised by the shining of light, the sound of the drum and the renewal of life

Christmas in Madurai

The Tamilnadu Theological Seminary, where I trained to be a minister, is in Madurai, the 'Temple Town of South India', nearly 200 miles away from my village. Madurai is a rural town surrounded by hundreds of villages and hamlets. The seminary seeks to raise awareness of the problems of rural people and encourages students to reflect on the relevance of the gospel to their situation.

Heartbreaking news frequently came to us from the villages around Madurai. The rural poor had no direct access to local authorities. They had to go through many middlemen and this often involved bribery. In one village alone in a particular year there were over 100 cases of female infanticide. The mother or midwife killed the baby as soon as it was born and found to be female. Either they put a paddy grain into the nostril or, if that failed, they fed the baby with the juice of a poisonous plant. They were surprisingly relaxed when they answered the queries of visitors, journalists and social workers. Their reasons deserve a little sympathy: 'We cannot protect these girls any more in a changing society. We do not have money to pay the dowry at the time of a promising marriage. And if the marriage fails, our daughters are handed over to worthless fellows at whose hands they die every day; it is better for them to die at birth than live for this.'

Similar news came from other parts of Tamilnadu, with the painful realisation that this heinous practice had been going on discreetly for a long time. A Tamil film powerfully demonstrated how a female child could be more resourceful and helpful than a boy for both the parents and society. The Government set up public cradles at police stations so that unwanted female children could be put in them and the Government would arrange care for them, but the programme was a failure. There are also cases of untouchability, sexual exploitation of the poor, encroachment on the land of the powerless by the powerful, as well as a lack of basic facilities like roads, houses, electricity and drinking water.

Apart from traditional events, one speciality of the seminary is its magnificent Advent Carol Service. Staff and students compose about ten new songs every year, relating the theme of the International Year to the problems of rural India. Practice starts well ahead and it is a great event, not only for the seminary community but also for the churches around. And it's not uncommon for members of other religious communities to attend. There are also visual presentations through a lantern competition, and one marvels at the creative imagination of people from different walks of life reflected in their artistic lanterns. Flying a hot-air balloon brings the programme to a close. Churches around are often inspired by it to arrange similar events in their own context.

In all these customs there are recurring themes. Here are some of them:

- Jesus the Great Liberator is chained to the altar in the church building and the church is called to liberate him.
- The Son of God – whose title is also Son of Man – is born on a street and identifies with unwanted children who are killed or abandoned.
- As Herod and the people of Jerusalem were troubled, so let those who oppress the poor and vulnerable have no

Jesus the Great Liberator is chained to the altar in the church building and the church is called to liberate him

peace until they repent and bow down before the vulnerable baby Jesus.

- Jesus risked death and persecution throughout his ministry so that all those who are victims of similar treatment can find new life and light in him.
- Love is the only power of a vulnerable child and by accepting such a child we discover the presence of God.
- Those who struggle find in God the power for survival and thus challenge all who are complacent and seek their own comfort.
- To aspire for power by the accumulation of wealth and destructive weapons leads to a demonic state of mind.
- Those who do not realise that their wealth and comfort are built on the spoils of the poor are criminals.
- The nativity scene provides a model of society where labourers, poor women, the educated class, the natural world, vulnerable children and the heavenly presence can together create a life of mutual sustenance and loving relationship.

At Madurai, these ideas are expressed in prose, and the poetic, emotive power of the songs and visual presentations is unparalleled.

Those who do not realise that their wealth and comfort are built on the spoils of the poor are criminals

In a seminary, students are also taught how the divine incarnation in Christ has been interpreted by theologians. This is not to accept totally what others have written. Overwhelmed by the challenges of their context they reflect upon it in their own way. Two such theological reflections stand out. One is the historical significance of the birth of Jesus: who is Christ in a multi-faith society? And the other is the geographical significance: was he born into a rural or urban situation?

Who is Christ?

The 2.5% of the population who are Christians in India live alongside Hindus (82%), Muslims (12%), Sikhs (1.75%) and a few other minority religious communities. The celebration of Jesus' birth does not evoke special curiosity in this context. Hindus celebrate the birthdays of gods, goddesses and saints; Muslims celebrate the birth of the Prophet Mohammed; and Sikhs honour the birth of Guru Nanak.

People of each faith respect Jesus in their own way. Hindus see him as one of the incarnations of God or as one of the greatest religious teachers. Muslims regard him as one of the greatest prophets, next to Mohammed who, for them, is the seal of all the cardinal prophets. For Sikhs he is one of the greatest Gurus through whom we have a glimpse of God and the ideal humanity. How do we present the uniqueness of Jesus Christ in such a context? What makes the celebration of Christmas special and distinctive in India?

Some Indian Christian theologians speak of Jesus as an *avatar*, a Sanskrit word meaning 'descent' – Jesus is the descending of God from heaven to earth. Sometimes this word is loosely translated as 'incarnation'. According to the *Vaishnava* tradition, one of the two major Hindu traditions, God Vishnu has made many descents, of which ten are the most important. Krishna, one of these descended forms, says in the famous text *Bhagavad Gita*, 'Whenever righteousness declines and unrighteousness increases I descend in order to save the righteous and destroy the wicked.' Krishna has been the most popular 'descent' in the *Vaishnava* tradition.

In Christ, God took real human form and so his coming is unique in Indian experience

Those who think of Jesus as an *avatar* emphasise what makes Jesus different from Hindu incarnations. Vishnu was incarnated in different forms – in animals and in semi-human and semi-animal gods, as well as in heroes like Krishna. But in Christ, God took real human form and so his coming is unique in Indian experience. Vishnu's 'descents' are enshrined in myths and legends, whereas Jesus was a historical figure. Jesus' life was also of a different quality: he reflected the heart of God and was himself a model for all people who, according to God's original intention, are made in his image.

This comparison is emphasised by popular Christian preaching. But it is not as simple as that. Thinking Hindus accuse these preachers of arrogance and, in any case, they think that limiting God's descents to only one incarnation makes the divine economy very stingy! But, on the other hand, their approach to religious pluralism in terms of 'one truth – many religions' does not help Indians to see what is distinctive in the coming of Jesus. There is no easy solution to this problem. The word *avatar* is also limited in meaning; it does not fully describe the incarnation of God (as Christians see it) or the Eternal Word in Jesus.

Furthermore, as we have already noted, the idea of *avatar* is accepted only in the *Vaishnava* tradition and not in the

Saiva tradition, which is most influential in southern India. According to *Saiva* theologians, God cannot take human form as it would involve going through the process of the chain of births and deaths that control human life. Instead, they extol the appearance (*theophany*) and disappearance of Siva in the forms of kings, sages and gurus. So theologians who are influenced by the *Saiva* tradition have tried to present Christ as the Guru. Like Siva teaching the souls of people through his immanent presence, Christ took the form of a human guru, helping to liberate the soul from its bondage to the consequences of previous existences. But all this is rather far-fetched.

It is indeed difficult to fit Mary's child into the Hindu pantheon.

Tell me the old, old story

More recently, the theological scene in India has been remarkably enriched by a new wave of reflections. This comes from the awakening of nearly 200 million people, formerly known as 'outcast', 'scheduled caste' and *Harijans* – 'people of God' or, more properly, 'the children of God Vishnu'. They have chosen for themselves a new name: *Dalits*, meaning 'those who are downtrodden and broken'. They are the age-long victims of untouchability, the offspring of the caste system who have been compelled to do all the dirty work, living on the outskirts of the villages.

Jesus is very special to *Dalit* Christians. They are neither dogmatic nor doctrinal in their approach to understanding Jesus. If he was the incarnation of the Eternal Word or the Son of God, by taking the form of a slave he identified with them in their slavery. Even if Jesus was born of a loose woman, as many of his day must have suspected, he is their friend, because, according to some myths of the past, *Dalits* were children of temple prostitutes. In this case, by adopting such a child, God has accepted all who, for generations, have carried the sin, guilt and wounds of their oppressors. They see Jesus as the Son of Man, the Human One, the representative of victims standing in solidarity with them to liberate them and, through them, to judge their victimisers. Their lullaby sung to the baby Jesus is the most authentic one, for it says that the salvation of others in India lies in Christians also identifying with the *Dalits*, coming down to their level and seeing God in a vulnerable child lying in a dirty manger.

Jesus is very special to Dalit Christians – by taking the form of a slave he identified with them in their slavery

What is becoming increasingly clear in understanding the birth of Jesus is that he cannot be taken up and isolated from his Jewish tradition. This mistake is made by many theologians in India and elsewhere. They take him from his religious tradition and try to fit him into their own religious categories to indigenise the Christian faith. Jesus is thus presented as a desirable person in the competing market of gods and gurus, and this diminishes the whole meaning of Christ's coming into the world.

No one should forget that Jesus was a Jewish child, the greatest gift of the Jewish tradition for the whole world. Jesus is significant for others only along with his tradition. Anti-Semitic attitudes and the traditional view of Christianity – that it superseded Judaism – have blinded many theologians to the universal significance of the whole story. It is a story of God taking a vulnerable community to be his instruments to humanise the whole world. The story of God's partnership with a group of slaves in Egypt – journeying with them in their struggles, in their successes and failures, in their hopes and frustrations, chiding and affirming them – provides profound insights for all peoples. No other religious tradition has preserved such a story so fundamental to their tradition, portraying God as the greatest companion and fellow sufferer of the victims of oppression. It pictures God in the midst of the outcast and untouchable, but also moving on, changing places, if those who were once victims become the oppressors. Jesus' birth in a poor working class family and his identification with those who lived 'outside the camp' (Hebrews 13.13) are a continuation of that same Jewish story. This story speaks to the heart of the 'untouchable' communities of India. The importunate rural masses need to know this story, the whole story, and nothing but the story.

No one should forget that Jesus was a Jewish child

Honouring the village

The angelic message to the shepherds was 'Unto you is born this day in the city of David a Saviour...' (Luke 2.11, AV). Was Jesus born in a city? Interestingly the Tamil translations have come up with a word meaning 'village'. This is significant for those who celebrate Christmas in Indian villages. Normally, we are taught in Sunday School that Jesus was born in Bethlehem and brought up in Nazareth. It is not a plain piece of history, as we will see.

David's original home was Bethlehem. The innocence and simplicity of the poor folk of Bethlehem is reflected in the way the elders welcomed Samuel's unexpected arrival with words of anxiety, 'Do you come peaceably?' (1 Samuel 16.4). David was looking after the sheep when he was anointed to be the king. Later on, he was anointed again and accepted as king by the people in Hebron, the highest town in Palestine (2 Samuel 5.1–3). At first, he remembered his origins. Even in his wanderings he held on to his passionate love of his village. On one occasion he longed for a drink of water from the well by the gate of Bethlehem (2 Samuel 23.15). Yet, later on, in his attraction to cities and programmes of urbanisation, he forgot his village, and this was detrimental for the future. First he captured Jerusalem, the city of the Jebusites, but this not only involved a heinous massacre of the lame and blind, but was the beginning of an oppressive and excluding policy: 'No one who is blind or lame is to come into the Lord's house' (2 Samuel 5.8, REB). Read this in the light of Jesus' healing the lame and the blind in the Temple after his triumphant entry into Jerusalem and cleansing the Temple (Matthew 21.14). This city came to be known as 'the City of David' (2 Samuel 5.9) and later 'the City of God' (Psalm 48.1,8; 87.3). It became the symbol of political and religious pride, but some of the prophets forecast that this pride would lead to disaster (for example, Jeremiah 13.9; 26.18; Micah 3.12).

A tradition developed that Jerusalem would become the centre of hope from which God's Word would go out to influence the rest of the world (Isaiah 2.3; Micah 4.2). But attention was also drawn to the forgotten village of David. After a warning about the instability of the 'walled city' we read:

> But you, O Bethlehem in Ephrathah,
> who are one of the little clans of Judah,
> from you shall come forth for me
> one who is to rule in Israel,
> whose origin is from of old,
> from ancient days.

(Micah 5.2)

This interesting ambiguity of the geographical identity of the 'anointed one' continues in the New Testament also. Matthew tells us nothing of the home of Joseph and Mary, but only that their baby was born in Bethlehem. The visiting astrologers of the east asked, 'Where is the child who has been born king of the Jews?' (Matthew 2.2). Perturbed by this query, Herod called together the chief priests and Jewish scribes, and asked them where the Messiah was to

Attention was also drawn to the forgotten village of David

be born. Quoting the verse from Micah, they replied, 'In Bethlehem of Judea'. And there is no indication when exactly the 'astrologers' visited the child in Bethlehem. Being warned of the decree of Herod for the massacre of all boys under the age of two, Joseph, Mary and the baby fled to Egypt and sought asylum there. After the death of Herod they were asked to go back to the 'land of Israel' (Matthew 2.20). Fearing Herod's son, the new king of Judea, and being directed in a dream, Joseph 'went away to the district of Galilee. There he made his home in a town called Nazareth'. Matthew notes that this was to fulfil the words spoken through the prophets: 'He shall be called a Nazarene' (Matthew 2.23, REB). For Matthew, despite this note, the fact that Jesus' family settled down at Nazareth was accidental, whereas for Luke it was their home town. Luke tells us that 'Joseph went up from the town of Nazareth in Galilee to Judea, to the city of David called Bethlehem, because he was descended from the home and family of David. He went with Mary, to whom he was engaged and who was expecting a child' (Luke 2.4–5). Was Bethlehem, as the birth place of Jesus, based on real history, or was it an interpreted tradition to fit the prophecy of Micah? Why did Mark and John omit the story of Jesus' birth altogether? It is significant that Jesus' birth place was never referred to in his lifetime.

Although John does not narrate the stories of the birth of Jesus, he includes an interesting comment on the geographical identity of Jesus in Nathanael's question, 'Can anything good come out of Nazareth?' (John 1.46). In John 7.40–44 we read of a debate about the Messiah's place of origin – Galilee or David's village of Bethlehem? 'So there was a division in the crowd because of him.' It is clear, therefore, that while the exact home of Jesus' family was uncertain, he was identified with Galilee and Nazareth, the most marginalised area of Palestine at that time. And it is significant that the rulers and people of Jerusalem were disturbed by his birth, that Jesus came to weep over the city which was the centre of political and religious authority, and that he was killed outside it. After his resurrection, Jesus urged his disciples to go to Galilee. The Great Commission to preach the gospel throughout the world was given on a mountain in Galilee (Matthew 28.19), thus belying the expectation that the Word of God would spring forth from Mount Zion.

This is an important insight for the rural masses of India. Gandhi said that India lives in villages. But in spite of more

Jesus was identified with Galilee and Nazareth, the most marginalised area of Palestine at that time

than a century of a polity based on democratic, social, republican principles, Indian villages are increasingly pushed to the background. One can detect a conspiracy drying up village resources and neglecting them in modernising programmes. This is the work of the wealthy, the bureaucrats and politicians. Consequently, poor people in the villages are forced to move into urban areas to work in industry and to live in hazardous conditions in the slums. Despite repeated calls, doctors and other high-level professionals are reluctant to live and work in villages. They prefer to settle in cities and towns where, ironically, 'open sewage canals are blocked by the building of private clinics'. Facilities abound in cities but villages are deserted. There is an 'urban psyche' which thinks that civilised life is possible only in cities. This is in spite of increasing pollution and the fast disappearance of a sense of community.

Jesus was born in a forgotten village and identified himself with the most backward area of his time. He challenged the accumulation of power and resources in urban centres. If it is true that the Eternal Word of liberation and enlightenment took human form in Jesus, the best place to realise his new-born presence is in those areas like Indian villages which are neglected and marginalised. According to the Bible, God always chooses the most vulnerable to be the primary location of his redemptive work. It follows, therefore, that the salvation of those who take pride in their historical and geographical identity lies in their coming down to the level of the poor in remote Indian villages like Parakkanvilai. In such places, in the midst of darkness and dirt, the child Jesus shines forth and calls all people to bow down before him and co-operate with him to create a new world.

In the midst of darkness and dirt, the child Jesus shines forth and calls all people to bow down before him and co-operate with him to create a new world

Open our eyes

Lord Jesus Christ,
you were born of the house of David –
a whole family, through many generations,
who passed down to you their traditions,
hopes and dreams,
in Bethlehem, 'the house of bread',
a small village like many we know.
In you we celebrate and affirm
the dignity of ordinary people:
the deeply held convictions of a mother,
the faith and insight of shepherds,
the perception of those who came from the east,
the dreams and visions of older people,
the meek who inherit the earth,
the prophetic challenge to wealth and power.
Your Kingdom has come near
our insignificant
and forgotten places.
Open our eyes to see you
and our lips to proclaim your presence.

Maureen Edwards

Immanuel

God of God...
only the sound of an infant
crying in the night,
a familiar, homely, human sound
like the sound of hooves on flagstones,
like the rattle of chains tethering cattle,
like the crunch of straw in the mouths of oxen,
like the rustle of hay tossed into a manger.

Light of Light...
only the light of a star
falling on an infant crib
like the light in a shepherd's lantern,
like the light in the eyes of a mother,
like the light in the learning of the wise men,
like the light that lightens each dawn.

Very God of very God...
only a pillow of straw
and an infant in rags and tatters
like the weather-worn blankets of shepherds,
like dusty, travel-stained garments of travelers,
like old cloths thrown to a beggar,
like cloths stuffed in a stable window
to keep the draught out and the cattle warm.

God is with us,
terribly, simply with us.
And the shadows of men (and women)
with arms outstretched to take Him
fall across the manger
in the form of a cross.

Chandran Devanesen, India
From *The Cross is Lifted*, Chandran Devanesen
© 1957 Friendship Press Inc.
Used by permission

Compassionate and Holy God,
We celebrate with joy your coming into our midst;
we celebrate with hope your coming into our midst;
we celebrate with peace your coming into our midst;
for you have come to save us.

By your grace we recognise your presence
in men and women
in all parts of your world;
by your power you set us free
from all that stands in the way
of your kingdom coming;
through your strength
our lives can proclaim joy and hope;
through your love
we can work for peace and justice.

You are the source of our being;
You are the light of our lives.

Based on a prayer from Latin America
© Christian Conference of Asia

5

Discovering Christ where people suffer

Sheila Cassidy

Isaiah 52.13 to 53.12
Matthew 1.18–25; 2.1–23
Luke 2.25–40
Matthew 25.31–46

Eat and drink together:
talk and laugh together:
enjoy life together:
but never call it friendship
until you have wept together.

An African saying

Room at the inn

I love Christmas and I have no sympathy with those boring people who complain that it's just commercial exploitation. I love every bit of it, from the lights in the high street and the wrapping of presents to the smell of turkey and the taste of Christmas pudding. I love getting Christmas cards, listening to carols and shopping for presents for friends and family, though I must admit to purchasing on a 'one for you and one for me' basis. Yes, of course I buy myself Christmas presents because, at sixty-two, I can no longer count on wonderful surprises and it would be terrible to spend Christmas feeling envious of others!

My best Christmases – the ones I have enjoyed most – are those in which I have spent myself for others. There is no joy like giving joy to others: of that I am sure.

My first teacher in how to spend Christmas was Father Michael Hollings, chaplain at Oxford when I was a medical student and a young doctor. The first time I was on duty around the Christmas period, Michael invited me to join him for Christmas dinner, and I was amazed to find a motley group of lonely women, widowers, ex-drug addicts and recently released convicts. Michael taught me well, although I was never as generous with the poor in mind and spirit as he was. I learned from him that one should never leave lonely people to spend Christmas on their own if an extra chair could be fitted around the table. He taught me, too, that one can have a merry time with people who are neither kin nor friends: what matters is that we should concentrate on making fun for others rather than demanding it for ourselves. If this sounds a bit puritanical, it's not meant to, because St Francis' famous aphorism – that 'it is in giving that we receive' – is true.

As a junior doctor, I frequently had to work over Christmas, and I can't remember one which I didn't enjoy. There was a tradition that the senior doctors came in to serve the patients' dinner and there was always much laughter with patients and staff. Christmas in hospital, of course, is always a poignant affair because most patients go home, if only for the day, so that those who remain are either too ill to move or have no one to go home to. It is Christmas, therefore, for the *anawim* (Hebrew – 'the poor'), the little ones and those marginalised by illness or oppression. The Bible makes it very clear that God has cast in his lot with the *anawim* and I have always found my hospital and hospice Christmases to be a deeply spiritual experience.

> *My best Christmases – the ones I have enjoyed most – are those in which I have spent myself for others*

The hidden Christ

I have deliberately spoken thus far about the ordinary, secular aspects of Christmas because it is there, as in the stable, that Christ is hidden. It is easy enough to feel 'religious' at beautiful services and on one's knees at the crib: but that is only one window on to the meaning of Christmas. The real meaning, as I understand it, is the incarnation of Christ among the poor, the downcast and the excluded. Jesus made this so clear, especially in the parable of the sheep and the goats:

> 'And when was it that we saw you sick or in prison and visited you?' And the king will answer them, 'Truly I tell you, just as you did it to one of the least of these who are members of my family, you did it to me.'

(Matthew 25.39, NRSV)

When I sit on the bed of a lonely old lady and hold her hand, it is Christ's hand that I am holding; when I spend half an hour or more listening to a young man struggling to come to terms with the fact that his wife will die, I am listening to a distraught and perhaps irrational Christ. The man's anger is God's anger, his pain God's pain, and often all I can do is to stand impotently at the foot of his cross, wishing I was somewhere else. Perhaps it's important to say that I don't always want to be there: hospital Christmases can be enormous fun, but they can also be very hard.

The key to sharing anyone's pain is empathy, the ability to enter into another's world as if it is one's own, but without losing the 'as if' quality. It is the 'as if it was one's own' that gives value to the person: that makes it 'empathy', not 'sympathy' (being sorry for). It's the 'not losing the "as if" quality' that makes it possible to do such work long-term: to do it year in, year out. Even then I find I have to make a deliberate effort to build fun into my life. This is why I buy myself Christmas (and non-Christmas) presents, why I live in as nice an apartment as I can afford, why I take holidays, and so on.

Perhaps one of the hardest things is to honour and cherish the Christ in ourselves: to accept and respect our own human need for love, for fun and for time out. There's a sense in which my liturgical seasons are jumbled up, out of step with the rest of the world. Any Christmas cards I send tend to get written after Christmas, and those that I receive are usually not displayed until Christmas Eve or later.

The key to sharing anyone's pain is empathy, the ability to enter into another's world as if it is one's own

Advent has usually passed before I've noticed it, but then it comes later in the post-Christmas calm, when I clear my house and try to make space for God in my life. Lent is a very different matter and comes when God sends it. Lent for me is not about fasting and penance but about shouldering the cross whenever it is my turn to carry it.

For me, the greatest hardship is mental exhaustion from receiving too much of people's pain. I have recently completed a four-year psychotherapy training course, so now I see men and women who have been abused or neglected as well as those who are dying. Each week I take on board the fury and anguish of an abused woman who also has cancer and, from time to time, I walk alongside young men and women facing death. This is, for me, the hardest: the fact that I cannot make them better – that their children will be motherless, that they will suffer and die.

An alternative Christmas

For many years, I worked in a hospice for the dying, so I am all too familiar with death. I have seen so clearly Isaiah's Suffering Servant in the faces of these people: the man (or woman) afflicted by suffering, 'acquainted with grief' (Isaiah 53.3). It's strange, but this sort of insight, while welcome in Lent, is not really wanted at Christmas.

If Christmas is about Emmanuel, God with us, then we should be prepared to think about bodily disease, decay and death

This year, I was asked to write a piece for the Christmas issue of a prestigious Catholic journal and I found myself writing an 'alternative' Christmas story in which Mary, mother of Jesus, instead of living to a gracious old age, died young of breast cancer. Not surprisingly the article was rejected: the editor showed it to other members of staff and they felt it was unsuitable. I knew what he meant: it seemed unnecessary to talk of such painful matters during the 'festive season'. The other thought was that it was somehow obscene even to think of the Mother of God as being 'defiled' by cancer. It would be all right to do it with the Christ story – we are prepared to think of Jesus as the Suffering Servant, one from whom we avert our gaze – but Mary, the spotless virgin, well, that's a different matter. The more I think about it, the angrier I feel, for if Christmas is about Emmanuel, God with us, then we should be prepared to think about bodily disease, decay and death. Christmas is always associated with images of the mother and child: pictures of a serene young woman and a clean, dry, happy baby. That's great, because babies are enchanting and there's something mysterious and awesome about the love between a woman and her child. Christmas is about happy families, but it is also about unhappy ones: families where Mother is dying of cancer or AIDS, families where mothers are drunk or drugged, neglectful or abusive. Is Christ not born into these families, just as much as he comes to the archetypal good Christian mother, father and two children?

I was thinking particularly of young women with breast cancer this year because I have, for the past three years, run educational support groups for patients suffering from this terrible disease. Our meetings are something between a seminar and a supper party: I ask each woman how her week has gone and we listen to each in turn. Some have had a good week, some a terrible one, vomiting after chemotherapy, or distressed by the hair loss which is often a side-effect of the anti-cancer drugs. There is much weeping and there is much laughter, and a wonderful growing compassion among the women for each other. After a break for coffee and cake (is this not a veritable 'breaking of bread', and is not the Lord among us?) I teach them for an hour. I explain to them what cancer is: a spontaneous or induced change in a cell's genetic material leading to uncontrolled growth. Cancer may look awful and smell worse, but it is not 'dirty'. It is not contagious and it is nothing to be ashamed of. It is a flaw in God's handiwork, his 'fault' if we must apportion blame.

Christmas is about happy families, but it is also about unhappy ones

When Mary and Joseph took Jesus to the Temple to present him as their first-born to the priest, Simeon prophesied in a way which must have made their blood run cold:

> **Simeon blessed them and said to Mary his mother, 'Look, he is destined for the fall and for the rise of many in Israel, destined to be a sign that is opposed – and a sword will pierce your soul too – so that secret thoughts of many may be laid bare.'**

(Luke 2.34b-35, NRSV)

A footnote in my New Jerusalem Bible says, 'As a true daughter of Zion, Mary will bear the sorrowful destiny of her race, with her Son she will be at the centre of this contradiction, where secret thoughts will be laid bare, for or against Jesus.' This makes me think of the women of Auschwitz, standing naked and humiliated as they walked to the gas chamber.

So how was Christmas in Auschwitz, I wonder? No joy there, nor laughter. When I think of Jews in Auschwitz, I wonder how it is that so many Christians have been, and are, so blind and stupid as to be anti-Semitic: against the Jewish people because they wear skull caps and celebrate different festivals. Or is it our pockets that they touch: are they hated because they are industrious, canny, clever businessmen who make more money than we do? I don't think I believe in original sin: certainly not in the sin of innocent babies before they have been baptised. But I know too well that we all carry within us the mark of Cain: the ability to discriminate, to dominate, to deceive, denigrate, and hate. That's the way we are: it's part of the human condition. I know too that the evil that men and women do is usually closely related to how they were treated as little children. There is an increasing body of research to show that if children are neglected or abused, they will most likely grow up wounded, and have difficulties making healthy relationships and being loving, respectful parents to their own children.

Mother and child

So now we have come back full circle to the mother and child, to the symbol of Christmas, to the incarnation of the Christ. Donald Winnicott, a child-psychotherapist, once wrote that 'there is no such thing as a baby', by which he meant that there is no such thing as a baby alone. Because an infant cannot survive uncared for, there must always be a *dyad*, a pair, a baby and a carer (usually the mother). It is from this 'nest' that we all grow, and how we grow is heavily dependent upon the quality of our mothering. This mothering, of course, is such an amazing marriage of heaven and earth: the love of the mother, sign of the love of God, incarnate in the very earthbound life of the child. The child is powerless, at the mercy of adults, as we are powerless, at the mercy of disease, the wilder elements, and of each other. It is as though the child's powerlessness is an icon of our own, and the mother's caring love is an icon of the divine.

It is so easy to sentimentalise, to trivialise this powerlessness and this love, but the reality is very different. Feeding a new-born baby is about cracked nipples and broken nights. It is about squalling red-faced infants soiling yet another nappy and demanding imperiously to be fed and held. Motherhood is a full-time, skilled, infinitely demanding, unpaid job. I often look at my pregnant friends and colleagues, ripe like pomegranates ready to burst, and think of the shattering labour they must undergo before

The child's powerlessness is an icon of our own, and the mother's caring love is an icon of the divine

their child is born and the exhaustion and daily washing which will haunt them during the years to come. The funny thing is, we never see Christmas cards of Mary changing Jesus' nappy, nor scolding him, not even feeding him, nor wearily trying to get a spoonful of mush into his petulant mouth. We never see her watching by his sick-bed, not even bathing a grazed knee. We do, of course, see her at the foot of the cross, anguished yet still serene – but not at Christmas: that wouldn't be fitting! That's human thinking for you: the parlour mentality. We must present a clean smiling face to the world, hide our wounds and our dirty underwear as if we were angels without any bodily functions or vulnerability.

I remember the nuns of my Convent school days in the 1950s who never ate in public and who never, it seemed, went to the lavatory. I contrast that 1950s ideal of purity and holiness with the death of my friend Ita Ford, the American Maryknoll sister, raped and shot dead in a white Transit van by Salvadorean soldiers. Another victim of this infamous and brutal murder was the American laywoman Jean Donovan who, like Ita, worked with orphans, the children of those killed by the military. What price Jean or Ita as Madonna with child? But perhaps they wouldn't look serene enough with so many mouths to feed.

Motherhood is a full-time, skilled, infinitely demanding, unpaid job

Every Christmas, my colleagues in our cancer support service, 'The Mustard Tree', hold a Christmas party for around seventy children and their mothers. Some of the mothers are members of 'Fighting Spirit', the group support programme which I run for younger women with breast cancer, while the other children have attended 'Jeremiah's Journey', our support programme for children who have lost a parent. One little girl comes with her aunt and her grandmother, because her mum 'Sally' died of breast cancer at the age of twenty-nine. Sally was in the very first 'Fighting Spirit' group, back in 1995. She was a lovely girl, clever, with a sparkling wit. She was a single mum, the father of her child having left her before the baby was born. There is no Joseph for these women, to love them, honour them and to provide the money, mow the lawn and mend the fences. I remember one day when the women in the group were sharing experiences, how Sally said that her little girl, then three, had asked, 'Mummy, will your booby (breast) grow back?' Sally explained that her breast was sick and that was why it had had to be cut off. In psychoanalysis, the in-depth 'talking therapy' devised by Freud and Melanie Klein, there is much talk of the 'good' and the 'bad' breast. The 'good' breast is the source of comfort and sustenance to the baby: his entire world before he is big enough to notice that it comes with his mother attached. The 'bad' breast is the empty breast which withholds his comfort and his dinner. One of the very first learning tasks of the new-born baby is to accept that the 'good' and the 'bad' breast belong to the same woman. As the child grows to maturity he or she learns that all people are a complex mixture of good and bad, of giving and withholding, just as the earth has its seasons of barrenness and fecundity.

Changing patterns

Our experience in prayer is very similar: consolation, that wonderful feeling that God loves one, is like the 'good breast'; but, for reasons we do not understand, we must learn to tolerate God's apparent withdrawal. When I was in Chile, I used to sit outside the Benedictine monastery above the city and watch the clouds come and go over the Andes. The mountains were my symbol of God: mighty and steadfast, beautiful and mysterious. Sometimes I could see them clearly and then, quite suddenly, they would vanish, playing hide-and-seek with me, as a mother does with her child. God loves to play hide-and-seek with us: one moment she is there, the next moment she is not and, like an abandoned toddler, we are frightened and bewildered. Little by little, however, we learn to tolerate it, to live with the memory of what has been and the hope of what is to come. As one gets older, one becomes accustomed to God's coming and going and learns to trust that light will follow darkness. This is basic spiritual teaching and I believe that, mostly, it is true.

God loves to play hide-and-seek with us: one moment she is there, the next moment she is not

For some people, however, this pattern simply does not hold true and, for better or for worse, my work is with them. They are the people for whom Christmas seems a hollow mockery of their pain, a mindless celebration by those who will not or cannot understand them. This, I suppose, is why I wrote my tasteless little 'Alternative Christmas' story in which Mary gets breast cancer and dies a year later in terrible pain. The trouble is, in my world, this story is more believable than the traditional story of the crib and the Magi, and it seemed a betrayal of my women not to tell it. I used a device of making Mary the patient because I thought it would hit people between the eyes. I wanted to alert them to the world of the *anawim*, the refugees, the homeless and the sick on their own doorstep.

One of the problems of today's 'First World Christian' is that we have 'compassion fatigue', especially concerning the victims of war and the homeless. I think I had more requests for money from the charities this Christmas than cards from my friends. They come now in every mail, whether or not I am paying them by a monthly standing order. I daren't read them because they make me feel so guilty, even though I give to charities on a regular basis. Perhaps my trying to make people care about young mothers with breast cancer is just another case of emotional blackmail. On the other hand, I was only trying to open people's eyes, not their pockets. Forgive me now if I get this out of my system. First, the human aspect, then the 'spiritual'.

The story goes like this. Breast cancer, usually, is a disease of older women, of women in their fifties and sixties who have reared their children. The public, family doctors included, do not expect women in their late twenties and their thirties to get breast cancer: but they do. Not many, but enough for me to run an eight-week group five or six times a year. It is sitting and listening to these women, becoming their friend and advocate, that has fired my passion. Because benign breast lumps are more common in younger women than malignant ones, some women are reassured by their doctors and sent away. When they are referred to the hospital, they may be referred as non-urgent cases and not seen for six to eight weeks. Sometimes this delay makes no apparent difference, but in those with aggressive disease, it surely must. To complicate matters, disease in younger women is harder to diagnose than in older women and diagnostic screening less reliable. When, eventually, these women are diagnosed, they are terrified, and rightly so. They know that they may die, that they may not live to raise their children. Whatever the future holds, they must live with their fear and vulnerability for many years.

Then, there is the treatment. Thank God, research has shown that the terribly mutilating radical mastectomy – which used to be the standard treatment when I was a medical student – is rarely indicated. Most women get away with having the lump removed, though there are still some who must have one, and, sometimes both, breasts removed. Then there is chemotherapy, dreaded by all. The medical reality is that chemotherapy is an important

One of the problems of today's 'First World Christian' is that we have 'compassion fatigue'

therapeutic development and saves many lives every year. The human reality can be very different if it brings in its wake a host of miserable and debilitating side-effects, from nausea and vomiting to hair loss. Last, but not least, is the castrating effect of chemicals and hormones which are essential to treatment because many breast cancers are hormone dependent. This is obviously a major issue if a young woman loses not only a breast, and with it her sense of femininity, but also her libido, her *joie de vivre* and her desire for her husband. This leads, in many cases, to difficulty in relationships and, in some cases, marriage breakdown.

Of course, it is not always like this. Caught early, breast cancer is potentially curable, and most women do well and are able to put the experience behind them.

So much for the woman: what about her children? How on earth can two- and three-year-old children understand why their mother is less available to them, why she cries and vomits? What are they to make of this new mummy who is bald, whose lovely hair has gone thin and lifeless? And what if she dies? A small child cannot understand the concept of death: he knows only that his 'good breast', his source of security, has abandoned him. Why, he asks, why? And on receiving no comprehensible answer, assumes that his mummy has gone away because she does not love him, because he is bad.

Women and men who lost their mother in early childhood have a much greater chance of depressive illness in adult life

Much research has gone into the impact in later life of the loss of a parent in early childhood and, sadly, many children are emotionally damaged. Women and men who lost their mother in early childhood have a much greater chance of depressive illness in adult life than do those who have not suffered such a loss. If the mother dies young, the impact upon the child depends in large measure upon subsequent care. Suppose the father marries again, how will the step-mother care for the child? When she and her husband have children of their own, will the child of the dead mother be disadvantaged? The story of Cinderella is, alas, not just a fairy story, because, not unexpectedly, many women find it difficult to love another woman's troubled child.

All are precious

Enough. What place, you may well ask, has this medical outburst in a devotional book, and a Christmas one at that? I make no apologies, however, because I am convinced that all that I have said is absolutely relevant to our theme. *El Shaddai*, the unknown, the transcendent God of the mountain, became *Emmanuel*, God with us, at the first Christmas. When the angels were heard to sing and the star appeared to the Magi, God became, if we are to believe Matthew 25.31–46, not only man but woman too, and although Jesus of Nazareth died, Jesus the Christ is with us until the end of time.

Sometimes, I think, we religious people forget what it means when we say that God became incarnate. To become incarnate means to take on flesh and thus become heir to all the ills and vulnerabilities of that flesh. As a woman and a doctor I am intimately aware of the bodily functions and the results of their breakdown and I see no 'unbaptised' areas of human life. By this I mean that God is 'in' not only our rising and lying down but all our daily activities. God bleeds with us, has 'flu with us and cancer too. The sick God needs to be acknowledged and honoured as much as – or more than – the God who is young and physically beautiful. This is what I mean by the spiritual aspects of illness: God is there, anaemic with menorrhagia, forgetful with Alzheimer's, dying of AIDS. All the world is holy ground, all people precious and to be honoured.

And lastly, lest I be seen as a pious kill-joy, let me tell you of my most recent Christmases. When the children of the patients, and the children who've lost a parent, have gone home clutching their teddy bears and we have vacuumed up the crumbs, I go home to my flat to prepare for my own Christmas. My late middle-age has been enormously blessed by the advent of Harry, my great-nephew, aged four-and-a-half as I write. Harry 'belongs' to me more than he would otherwise have done because his mother has no partner, so all available members of the family are involved in his upbringing. I, as a childless woman, have been given a child to love, to buy presents for and to take on holiday. As the only member of the family who is earning, I am involved in his current and future welfare in a way which warms my heart. I think to myself that, when I am sixty-seven, Harry will be ten, and what fun I'll have with him if his mother and he are still living nearby. I see too how Simeon could utter the *Nunc Dimittis*: 'Now, Master, you are letting your servant go in peace...' (Luke 2.29, NJB). The fact of a new young life growing up makes the notion of my own eventual departure bearable. It is perhaps because of Harry that I am especially alert to the needs of his mother and therefore the needs of all young women under stress.

All the world is holy ground, all people precious and to be honoured

Perhaps Christmas could become a special time to honour and cherish single mothers as they struggle to take care of the Christ Child for us.

Christ, our guest

Lord Christ,
born again for us
each Christmas,
help us to recognise you
among the sick
and the marginalised.
Give us courage to
open our doors
and take you in,
even when we think
we have no space
for another guest.
Let there always be room
at the inn.

Sheila Cassidy

Gifts to offer

Inspire us, God of all that is good and lovely,
to bring to you our gifts of gold, beauty and fine things,
the best we have,
that we may celebrate their value together
as a family from which no one is excluded.

Make us whole, loving God.

Move within us, God of prayer,
that we may offer to you the incense
of our longing and emptiness
so that you may fill us with new life and hope,
renewed vision and energy.

Make us whole, loving God.

Come to us, suffering God,
that we may bring to you the myrrh of our isolation
that you may soothe our pain
with the balm of your healing touch.
Let us not hide away from the world
but, with you, enter into solidarity
with others who suffer and grieve
and find strength in helping one another.

Make us whole, loving God.

Come to us this Christmas, O Emmanuel:
dispel our darkness with the comforting softness
and profound beauty of your twilight.
Heal our woundedness
and bring your peace to our troubled world. Amen

Maureen Edwards

6

Discovering Christ in the South Pacific islands

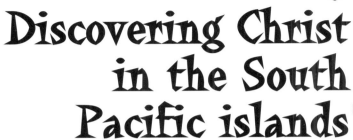

Bernard Thorogood

John 1.1–14
1 John 1.1–4
Hebrews 1.1–4

The Word dwells among us. It is as though the reef is our home, where ocean and island meet. The more we appreciate this interweaving, the readier we are to be challenged and healed by the Word of God.

Bethlehem reef

There is a sound that lingers. A distant roar. background hum. It is the sound of the waves on the reef. At points it is close to the island and at others far away On some days the sound is low and unnoticed, on other powerful. It is the constant reminder that each island ha this margin and beyond is the ocean, immense, stronge than any boat, unpredictable. The reef is a bulwark, a lin of defence, for there the waves crash and spen themselves. The coral of the reef is the meeting point c land and ocean; solid and hard, it lives only in the wate constantly developing, building over the centuries an battered by storms. The sound of the reef speaks of fragilit and strength, of distances and waves, of the edge where th land drops down into the depths of the ocean.

This memory is a starting point for our thinking about th meaning of Christmas, where we approach the grea mystery of the coming of God into the world in a human life It will always be a mystery. We cannot, in this life, know th whole being of God, nor the whole eternal purpose in ever part of creation. Nor can we probe into the mind of Jesu Christ as a modern psychoanalyst might do. How did th limited knowledge of a man operate alongside the 'ligh inaccessible hid from our eyes'? And what wonder and glor was poured into a baby, so fragile, so unknowing? Humbl' we approach that place at which the world of eternity me the world of dust, pain, joy and tears – the 'Bethlehem Ree – where the ocean of God touched the island of our lives.

That sense of mystery and immensity comes through th opening passage of John's Gospel, one of the greate: expressions of Christian faith that have come down to us. is poetry, philosophy and theology all bound up together. I John 1.1–14, the Evangelist brings together the creation c the universe and that family in Bethlehem, the ocean an the island. John's insight led him to use the term *Logos* t indicate the outward expression of God towards the worlc God's body language, which theologians call the sel revelation of God. In the Polynesian language which I usec the translator kept it as *Logo*. In English it became 'Word But even that seems inadequate, for a word may be just convenience or a tool. Here, at the start of John's Gospe we have the 'Word' as God in action, God speaking, Go creating. The 'Word' is not separate from God, but is Go touching time.

The sound of the reef speaks of fragility and strength, of distances and waves, of the edge where the land drops down into the depths of the ocean

ohn tells us that this is something which is always true bout God and not just the Bethlehem event. There was no eriod in the history of the universe when God was absent r asleep or unconcerned or mute. Always the Word was ctive, and in the life of humanity the Word has always ome as light. Today we are learning slowly about the istory of physical life on this planet, and the long slow rocesses by which the simplest cells developed from lime into primitive sea creatures and eventually into fish nd so on. We know only a little of that history but what we o know is marvellous, and in it all we can see the active nergy of the creating God. In our human life that creative ift of God is what John calls 'light'.

erhaps we can say that we are animals lighted by God, for hysically our bodies are just like those of mammals. But here is something more, some awareness and striving, ome dreaming and planning, some loving, creating, aughing and talking, which is what makes us human. So he creating God makes us creators too. And it is that light f human-ness that comes in the person of Jesus. The light, ll that creative energy of God, all that longing for wholeness, is given to the world in the person of the child f Bethlehem. Why? John answers us, so that we too may ecome fully the children of God that we were destined to e (John 1.12–13). We are called to live in God's world, usting in God's way, so that we may fulfil God's purpose. he world then becomes the home in which we all have to earn to live as one family. I think we have not yet got very lose to this longing of God.

o John comes to the great verse 14, which we can use as summary of the whole gospel of Christ. 'So the Word ecame flesh; he came to dwell among us, and we saw his lory, such glory as befits God's only Son, full of grace and 'uth' (NEB). The glory was a family in a stable in a country own of a neglected province of an empire that faded long go. It was a glory that included a crown of thorns: a glory hat not all could see. So we can speak of the glory of God eiled in flesh – not just clothed in flesh but also hidden in esh. We saw his glory – 'we' is the little company of ollowers who were able to see in the man of flesh and lood something so lovely, so powerful, and so life-giving hat they saw God's glory too, when all those around could nly see the heretical preacher from Galilee. But the 'we' is lso us, the whole company of the people who meet in hrist's name, for we have seen in the man who was born Bethlehem the amazing welcome, the home that is God.

There was no period in the history of the universe when God was absent or asleep or unconcerned or mute

The bundle of life

When you live on a small island there is every reason to learn how to live as part of a community and not be a loner. Your family will have links right across the island population and you are likely to have a dozen aunts and uncles. Young children belong to the whole family rather than to their natural parents. The strengths and weaknesses of an individual cannot be hidden when all the men are fishermen and watch each other's catch, or when all the women weave baskets and can see who does the neatest job. The decisions which shape the future tend to be community decisions even if they are actually pronounced by a chief. So religion is also about the life of the whole community. I believe and I worship, not because some vision or conversion has come to me individually, but because I am part of a village which believes and worships. This pattern of a close community could be repeated in thousands of villages across the globe.

You can imagine that such a way of life can be constricting just as it can be beautiful. There is not much room for the brilliant individual, or for great achievement in art or commerce or education. There is not much room, either, for dissent, but for holding on to life in a place with small natural resources. It reminds us all how strong is a sense of community, a sense that has been lost most to people of the industrialised world for a century.

The opening of the first Letter of John (1 John 1.1–4) reminds us of the opening of the Gospel, and it is likely that the same John wrote both. These opening verses are vivid, so that we can almost hear the writer pouring out the words in a rush of eagerness. His theme is the Word of life, that 'Word' of God once more. But here the writer tells us that he saw it, looked on it and touched it with his hands, that he was present with the man Jesus and is telling about the great experience of his life. At the time when this was written there were strange ideas circulating about Jesus. Some said that he was not genuinely a man, but only appeared like one. That was the story of many ancient myths, an appearance of a god in the shape of an animal or a human figure. But John sets out to demolish that theory. We saw him and touched him and knew him each day; he was flesh and blood like us. So at Christmas we can say that this was a real birth, a birth with pain, and a real baby who yelled and squealed and opened his eyes to see a very real mother.

At Christmas we can say that this was a real birth, a birth with pain, and a real baby who yelled and squealed and opened his eyes to see a very real mother

John declares the purpose of this coming of the Word of Life. It is that 'you also may have fellowship with us; and truly our fellowship is with the Father and with his Son Jesus Christ' (verse 3). Here we touch one of the great words of the New Testament. It is the word *koinonia*, which is translated in English as 'fellowship' or 'common life' or 'communion'. It is the same word that we find in the Blessing, 'the fellowship of the Holy Spirit'. Another use of it is in Acts 2.44 where the believers had all their property in common', *koina*. So John sees the object of preaching the gospel to be a sharing in a common life which the believers share also with God.

How do we experience this? The quick answer is to say, 'church'. That is the community in which we are at one in our prayers, our study, our service and our praise. It is the community where we are known and trusted and forgiven. In this community we are at one with believing people of every race and language and generation. Here we are 'in communion' with the saints, teachers and the faithful of past ages. This is the common life of the people of God.

But the reality is not so clear as that. The community of believers is broken up into congregations, many of which have little care for other congregations but are extremely busy with their own local affairs, so that there is little sign of a common life. The community is also broken into ethnic groups which stay together and seldom cross the language barrier. We know also the fractured nature of the community in the denominational labels we carry. There are barriers between us even at the holy table of the Lord. So the common life is not clearly visible in the Church as we know it, and that is a Christian's sorrow.

When we do see the common life we know something very precious. Once in a Polynesian village the people gathered for prayer at 2.00am and stayed there in the meeting house for an hour, a kerosene lamp hanging from a rafter, and the sound of prayers matching the night breeze in the coconut palms. Why were they there? Because a young woman of the village was, at that exact hour, in London sitting her final law exams at university. She was part of her community at home. They were wholly at one with her. Their village became a community of the Spirit, and we saw the common life of the children of God.

To make the common life visible and actual every day is the calling of the Church, for this is what draws the lonely and the frightened and the lost out of their darkness and

John sees the object of preaching the gospel to be a sharing in a common life which the believers share also with God

into God's light. It is our calling in every congregation, that we become sharers with one another, and between congregations, that we end all sense of rivalry, competition or mutual distrust, and embrace one another in all our sorrows and our joys. That is a Christmas calling, 'that the joy of us all may be complete' (verse 4).

Prophetic voices

In several Pacific Islands there is a similar tradition. Talking with an elder I heard the following story. 'Long before the missionaries first arrived, our people knew that something great was going to happen. We were used to the arrival of people from neighbouring islands, both for peace and for war, and we spotted their brown sails on the horizon. But the old prophets said that a different boat would come, with white sails, carrying white people and that would be a great change for all our community, a new doorway in life. So when that ship did appear and when it carried white-skinned people, we knew that the day had come and we welcomed them. They were the first missionaries.' It is a story often told, and it has certainly been elaborated over the years, but behind it is something of great importance. The coming of the Word of God is not unprepared.

Taken all together the prophets provided a road along which people could travel towards the presence of God

'God spoke to our ancestors' (Hebrews 1.1–4). The Word of God was active then, back in the distance of human memory. And it was the same God, whom we know in Jesus Christ, who was speaking. But then 'he spoke in fragmentary and varied fashion through the prophets' (REB). It was fragmentary since each one saw a little of the truth of God, not the whole; and it was varied since each one emphasised a distinct aspect of the holiness and glory of God. But, taken all together, the prophets provided a road along which people could travel towards the presence of God. So, says the writer, we come to this present age when 'God has spoken to us by a Son.' The road has reached its goal, for in Jesus we are in the presence of God.

As we experience different human societies and faiths, we are bound to ask whether this sense of a preparation for Christ is strictly a matter of the Jewish tradition alone, or whether it has a much wider aspect.

The answer is surely that the prophetic voice was heard and is heard in every part of the human family. 'The true light which enlightens everyone, was coming into the world' (John 1.9). God's Word is God's nature and did not begin at

Bethlehem. Wherever people have approached the deep realities of life, wherever people have offered their hearts in adoration of the highest, wherever a voice of conscience and generosity and forgiveness has been heard, wherever the claims of the downtrodden and the handicapped have evoked a response – there the Word of God has been speaking and the way has been prepared for Jesus Christ. And that is in every age and every part of the human family. Yet Jesus himself came out of the Jewish tradition and not from any other. So I would see the Old Testament as the direct road leading to Christ and the myriad other prophetic voices as more indirect, harder to discern, but truly there.

A second question then presses us. Why is it that so much preparation did not enable more people to welcome Jesus Christ? As we read the Old Testament we hear the repeated complaints of the prophets that their voice was not heard, not received. Their preaching did not reach everyone and many who did hear it turned aside and rejected the message.

The prophetic voices were not persuasive enough, persistent enough, charismatic enough, to draw the whole people towards the reality of God. So the worship of the Temple, by the time of Jesus, had become almost a barrier on the path to God rather than a highway. The Jews had been led, over centuries, to expect something very different from Jesus, a Messiah who would be a hero, a victor, a king. A great tradition had come to be wrongly applied, partly because of the political struggles of the nation. The reality of Jesus was something else, unorthodox in word and deed, offending all the powers of the land, and so, hard for people to recognise.

Something more than a prophetic voice was needed. And all over the world more is needed than the hints of God's light and truth that reach all seekers for God. So 'in these last days he has spoken to us by a Son ... He is the reflection of God's glory and the exact imprint of God's very being' (Hebrews 1.3). The light is shining, the man Jesus is the seal of God, the true image of God. That is the Word in flesh which all may hear and see and adore. Not a sermon or a suggestion or a spasm of conscience or a book of law, not a liturgy or a theology, but a person. It is as though God says, 'Through the centuries I have tried to touch your hearts through all those prophecies and all those signs, but you have not yet grasped the reality. Now, here I am. See me, touch me, here are the scars of the nails. And believe.'

Not a sermon or a suggestion or a spasm of conscience or a book of law, not a liturgy or a theology, but a person

Advent

The islands where I lived for most of my Pacific ministry are known as the Cook Islands. It is an honourable name but suggests that the islands hardly existed before that great Yorkshire man put them on the map. In fact no memories of him remained. It was the early missionaries who were remembered. The annual celebration of their arrival was the great public holiday of the year, in October and is still called Gospel Day.

On that day, schools were closed and from each village crowds gathered, by truck and bus and on foot, to one of the larger church grounds. The sellers of watermelon and peanuts were out in force. A brass band tootled. Guitars were strummed. Choirs started up their strident chants. Prayers and hymns began the celebration and then each village presented a biblical drama of their own invention, in glorious Technicolour. We might see Samson and Delilah or Pharaoh and Moses. One year we saw Elijah on Mount Carmel calling on fire from heaven, which turned out to be a flaming pot of kerosene sliding down a guide wire from the top of a coconut palm to the altar. And we might see Paul being shipwrecked or the Nativity or the Resurrection. In each drama the children played a major part, with marching songs of their own and bright costumes. It was a community celebration of the history of faith, in honour of that day when the light of the gospel arrived.

So it was their Advent. Jesus had come to them. In fact it meant more to the people of the islands than 25 December which always seemed to me a rather imported, European style occasion. This is perhaps how Christmas is properly made indigenous, how the coming of Christ to us is made the key to our faith year. In many places it is far more difficult to point to a single date in history when the Christian message reached our land, for the time is way back, centuries ago. But there may well be a personal date which we remember when we first knew the reality of God's grace in Jesus Christ. We can keep that anniversary as an Advent day.

Yet in the islands the celebration was perhaps just a little too happy, too bland, too splendid a holiday, to carry all the meaning of Advent. For there is pain also. The Gospel reminds us that 'the light shines on in the dark, and the darkness has never mastered it' (John 1.5). 'He was in the world; but the world, though it owed its being to him, did not recognise him. He entered his own realm, and his own

There may well be a personal date which we remember when we first knew the reality of God's grace in Jesus Christ. We can keep that anniversary as an Advent day

would not receive him' (John 1.10–11). This has been true ever since. The welcome for Jesus has not been unanimous, even in places like Polynesia where there was a mass movement into the Church. We know in our own lives that, as we rejoice to recognise him, there is darkness still in our attitudes and prejudices and self-concern. So the birth of Jesus in Bethlehem or in Polynesia or in your own life is challenge and judgement as well as wonder and joy. This is not to condemn all the merrymaking of Christmas, but to remind us that in the little country town there was not only the song of the angels but also the sword of a murderous monarch.

Each island had its own history and among the strangest is the story of the coming of the gospel to Nukulaelae, a small atoll in the group now known as Tuvalu. The story begins in Manihiki on 22 April 1861, when a canoe set out for Rakahanga, just forty kilometres to the north of Manihiki. The Rakahanga people had been attending a church service in Manihiki and were going home, six men, two women and a child. It was a double canoe, the two hulls lashed together with a rough deck across them. They were in sight of Rakahanga when the wind changed and powerful gusts drove them away from the shore; they thought that they should try to return to Manihiki. Night overtook them, out of sight of land. In the morning, there was no sight of land. They decided to steer to the south, for they had few provisions and needed a sight of land quickly. But the days passed and the horizon was empty. After two weeks they had a glimpse of land, but the wind and the currents carried them away. They had to bale constantly. After more drifting they were down to six coconuts, and they were much weaker, but then the catch of a shark raised their hopes again. One of the party, Elekana, was a deacon and he led prayers every morning and evening, and on Sunday read from his Bible. This drift went on for eight weeks, and then land was sighted once more. They hoisted their sail and soon heard the breakers on the reef. A shower of rain brought them refreshment. They were tossed in the breakers, the canoes were smashed, but they were thrown onto the beach. Of the original nine persons, five survived, one of them being Elekana. Local people soon found the exhausted group, and the dead bodies which they buried, and brought food and clothing and offered hospitality. As they were revived and told their story, Elekana took the initiative in speaking about the gospel, for he found that his own language could be understood. There, on Nukulaelae,

The birth of Jesus in Bethlehem or in Polynesia or in your own life is challenge and judgement as well as wonder and joy

he stayed and became the teacher of the people. The drift voyage had carried these islanders nearly 3 000 kilometres.

So here was an Advent which seems a total accident, wholly unplanned. But God's preparation was surely in the character of the islanders. It was their fortitude and faith which enabled Christ to be preached; it was the kind of people they were which ensured that their survival was creative. We do not see the intervention of God so much in a particular direction of the wind, the waves and the currents as in the characters of the people. It is the way of the Holy Spirit. For many centuries religious people of many faiths have seen the hand of God intervening in the natural forces – he thunders, he brings a drought, a flood, a storm at the critical time and so directs events. That now seems an inadequate view of God's action in the world, for causes and effects in nature are much better known today. But the formation of people is surely the clearest way in which God, the Holy Spirit, affects our lives. We are touched by others who have been influenced by Jesus Christ. So our Lord comes to us in faithful people, and at Christmas this is the Bethlehem we know and celebrate.

There is another message in the story of Elekana. What a fragile, risky business it was, a canoe on the ocean, drifting, powerless; all of them could have disappeared without trace. The route of the Word of God into our lives is through just such a risky process, just a baby, tender, defenceless and open to all the dangers of sickness, violence and oppression. Why should this be so? It must be because it is the character of God that God does not come to us in the clothing of power and wealth, security, command and headline-grabbing, but in the unnoticed, the risky, the vulnerable. It is not the way of the mass media but the way of the human heart.

Back to the reef

Where the ocean meets the island is not a neat ruled line. The reef is jagged, wayward, with its own inlets and promontories. It is varied in colour and shape. The most striking view of it is from the air, where we can see the dark blue depths and then the turquoise, the green, the copper, the cobalt in all the convolutions of coral. The boundaries between the divine and the human are not a straight line on the map of human society and we are often at a loss to say that here God is active and there God is absent, or that here we are dealing in eternal things and

God does not come to us in the clothing of power and wealth, security, command and headline-grabbing, but in the unnoticed, the risky, the vulnerable

there our concern is temporal. In fact the two are constantly interwoven, so that the daily sunrise speaks of eternal love, and the distant song of the angels is a word spoken to today's wars. Sacred and secular are not to be separated by any temple wall or priestly vocation. The Word dwells among us. It is as though the reef is our home, where ocean and island meet. The more we appreciate this interweaving, the readier we are to be challenged and healed by the Word of God.

Can you hear that roar of the waves on the reef, and feel the spray on your face?

The daily sunrise speaks of eternal love, and the distant song of the angels is a word spoken to today's wars

At Bethlehem Reef

At Bethlehem Reef the waves are crashing,
the foam is flying in the wind;
that great mass of the ocean –
which is always beyond us,
out of our grasp,
stronger and longer than us –
breaks and trembles and spills
on the edge.

At Bethlehem Reef there is dazzling light
where sun and water and rock collide;
Light of angels, Light of life,
Light in our darkness,
Light for all who are born in our world.

God of light and life and word and flesh,
we do not always know your coming;
we are self-absorbed, small-visioned.
May we know you at Christmas.
Break through to us,
shake our defences,
and let your ocean of love
flow across the rock and sand of daily life.

Bernard Thorogood

7

Discovering Christ through prayer

Melvyn Matthews

1 Samuel 1.1 to 2.10
Luke 1.5–80
Luke 2.22–40

*Prayer is a constant inner music which is
playing within us and within the created
order. We need to rediscover this music.
There is within each one of us a space where
this music can be heard, a silence within
which it is played.*

Prayer is really a discovery of your own inner incompleteness. To continue in prayer means to continue to trust that this incompleteness is God's and only God's. Prayer means trusting that your sense of emptiness is not purposeless but fertile. In one sense each one of us is an emptiness, an open space within which God speaks his word. The great difficulty with prayer is trusting that this is the case and expecting, indeed allowing, God to speak within your incompleteness. Spiritual discipline consists of working to keep this emptiness for God and God alone. To pray is to live positively with this sense of incompleteness and to resist trying to fill it with other things. These other things – pleasure, fulfilment, distractions of various kinds – will then displace God and so become competitors for our allegiance to God. The Old Testament calls these competitors 'idols'.

The darkness and emptiness of our own incompleteness is very difficult to bear but it is essential for us to do so if we are to be faithful. Faith in God means not filling our own incompleteness with idols. The temptation is to fill that space with our own speech, our own 'talking'. But it is this space within us which is the very point at which we may hear the word of God and the point at which that word becomes 'born' in us. If that 'birthing' is to occur then we have to keep the faith and keep the space for that for which it was made, God.

Prayer is really a discovery of your own inner incompleteness

It is not quite enough, when talking about prayer, to say things like 'We must keep ourselves open to God's presence', or 'We must allow ourselves to become aware of God', as some writers on prayer have done. We are talking about more than 'awareness', or even 'presence' at this point. 'Awareness' is a modern category and derives from the personalistic and experience-based philosophies with which this age abounds. In many ways such language is the fruit of the self-absorption which is characteristic of today. We may well become aware, but if God is who we claim him to be then it would also be true to say that we may not become aware simply because the reality of God is too great for us. Indeed it would be more faithful to the reality of God to say that, in the normal run of things, we do not become aware of God simply because talk of 'awareness' risks reducing God to the level of the human. God's reality may – indeed probably should – blind or overwhelm us. It may also be so great and so different as to fill us with fear and so make us feel compelled to disengage ourselves from

t. Rilke, the German poet, spoke truly when he said that beauty is but the beginning of terror.

It is also true to say that to describe prayer in terms of 'awareness' is limited because it is static. It talks about prayer as if we were aware of the presence of another person, or as if we were looking at a painting or a landscape. The relationship between the person praying and God is much more dynamic and, to use a modern word, 'interactive' than that. We do not become aware of God without something actually happening to us. As we pray, his word becomes born in us and may bear fruit. We may not be 'aware' of this, but that is what is happening. There is an activity here with which we may co-operate or not: there is a word being spoken which we may hear or ignore.

All of this is to indicate how I believe that a number of influences have been at work which mean that our understanding of prayer has become very limited and impoverished. It has been reduced to the level of 'asking and getting' by the mechanised and contractualised view of life which is prevalent in modern society. We need to bear that in mind when talking or thinking about it. In particular we need to bear that in mind when we read the accounts of 'visitation' to the personalities involved in the biblical narratives of the birth of Jesus. These narratives are important for our understanding of prayer because they are narratives about people who were aware of their own incompleteness and were even more aware of the immensity of God, but were content to live with that and allow their incompleteness to be overwhelmed and their inner space to be filled with the spokenness of God. They allowed God to be born within them in various ways.

A number of influences have been at work which mean that our understanding of prayer has become very limited and impoverished

Godspace

But speaking about prayer in this way may immediately puzzle or confuse. So before we move on to consider the narratives surrounding the birth of Jesus and their relationship to prayer in more detail, it is important that we spend a few moments trying to re-envision our understanding. Let me try and do this using the imagery surrounding the word 'space'.

I once had a friend who was an architect. He was also my churchwarden and so I would sometimes go down to his office, perhaps during the lunch hour, and discuss church business with him there. This also gave me the opportunity to ask him about his work and what he felt to be important about it. He was a very interesting and thoughtful man and used to say that it was his job to create spaces for people. He took this seriously and thought carefully about what sort of spaces would make people happy or unhappy. He was unhappy when he had to design shopping malls or bus stations and other large-scale, impersonal buildings which he believed diminished people or gave them little sense of worth or beauty. Eventually he left to set up his own practice so that he could control what he designed. He said that he felt that spaces and the way we inhabit them were important and had some sort of 'religious' or 'spiritual' dimension. Some spaces enabled you to live more deeply, more spiritually, if you like, as a person. Others did not.

I was struck by what he said and began to realise that there were some spaces which released in us more of a sense of wonder than others. Spaces which have beauty and proportion about them, more simplicity and clarity of line, evoke more of a sense of transcendence than those which are crowded or which push you in upon yourself. Some of the effect of this can be felt when we drive along a country road and then suddenly emerge into one of England's wide and ancient high streets. We experience a sense of relief and arrival, a settling of our being, and we want to stop and pause. This is particularly marked as you drive along the old London road and suddenly do a double bend and arrive in the high street at Marlborough where beautiful eighteenth century houses with big windows line the sides of the market place. The soul welcomes such an arrival. Other sorts of spaces speak to people. Many have been deeply struck by the elegance and simplicity of the space created by the Millennium Dome at Greenwich and have wanted to stand in it without the clutter of the many 'zones' representing different areas of human endeavour or achievement. The different rooms and terraces of the Alhambra in Granada speak of the need for calm and bring a silence to the soul. Spaces such as these resonate within the depths of our being and remind us that we have a space within us which maybe has been lost under the pressures of modern living.

Each year in the cathedral in which I work, we remove the chairs from the nave during the month of January. This is partly for cleaning purposes and to allow a number of promenade concerts to take place in the great open space which is left, but it also serves a profoundly spiritual function. People come into the cathedral and stand and

Spaces which have beauty and proportion about them, more simplicity and clarity of line, evoke more of a sense of transcendence than those which are crowded or which push you in upon yourself

marvel at the beauty of the nave in a way which they do not, indeed cannot, when all of the chairs are present. The great Gothic pillars come from the ground in a way which has been hidden for most of the year, indeed they appear to grow out of the floor in a natural way. The floor seems to move beneath you and the eye is drawn more surely to the great crucifixion above the altar at the east end. The space which is created enlarges the heart so that you want to sit and be in that space and allow it to speak to you in a way which you cannot at other times. This space resonates with your interior space and causes it to grow and be so enlarged that you become aware of your soul as an opening for the divine, as a space within which the word of God may be spoken. You find yourself waiting in the silence for the word to be born in your innermost depths. Your emptiness is filled.

In the modern age we have become much more self-conscious and so aware of our need for space. When I was the Director of a residential conference and retreat centre, I used to ask people why they had come and what they were looking for. So many of them said, 'I just want some space'. Modern ways of living and working exclude space from our lives and crush or destroy that interior space which is so necessary for our spiritual health. Modern life is crowded and quick and noisy, such that we feel we have to keep up with the speed at which everything else is going. The incessant demand for achievement of one kind or another affects more and more people. Even the traditional so-called 'caring professions', like nursing or church ministry, are affected by these trends. But eventually we are diminished by this way of life. Or at least we know we are diminished when we become aware of what has happened. One of the difficulties is that many people think this is how we should be and do not question what is happening to them until some tragedy or some crisis occurs to make them ask questions.

Like my architect friend I do not think that this need for space is merely psychological. Our deeply felt need for space is an indication of a greater and deeper need for God. We are all created with the capacity for knowing and loving God. We have within us a Godspace within which God will speak his word. This 'Godspace' has to be re-found and lovingly preserved within us. It has to be reached for in an age which forgets or smothers any sense of interior openness. It has almost to be fought for in a climate which regards such awareness as totally personal,

You find yourself waiting in the silence for the word to be born in your innermost depths. Your emptiness is filled

private and idiosyncratic. But when we do reach for it and allow it to flourish we become more confident believers and happier and more settled, purposeful people because we become slowly but surely aware that God is doing the living within us. Discovery and acceptance of our Godspace sets us free to be, to believe and to act for others in a way which nothing else can do.

In order to help you to understand this way of talking about prayer, and to rediscover your 'Godspace', it might help you if you engage, every now and again, in one or two short and simple exercises. Just as the pianist's fingers or the athlete's legs and lungs need regular exercise in order to be capable of their best, so the human soul needs Godspace exercises in order to preserve its capacity to be open to the reality of God. Some people call such exercises 'heartwork'. All of us need to practise this 'heartwork' regularly to enable us to become and to remain fully human beings, that is human beings who are fully aware of their capacities for openness to God. Effectively all prayer is an exercise in openness to God, but before the words come it is important to prepare the space in which these words can be said and have their true meaning.

One such exercise might be to find a quiet space. This can be anywhere from a church to a room in your home. It should be quiet and uncluttered. A walk alone in a city park or in the countryside might be as good if you cannot find a quiet space in your house. Above all find somewhere where you can simply be without interruption and can be inside yourself without stress or pressure. Hopefully also this space is one in which you can sense the beauty and wonder of creation. When you have found that space, reflect for a while on how you feel once you are there. What does it do to you? What does it open up inside your soul? Make a mental note of your reactions. You may feel freer or lighter. Ask yourself what this lightness of being is for. What are you going to do with it? You may feel troubled. If the sense of space frightens you, even a little – and it may do – then ask yourself why this is. Allow yourself to be in that space, without distractions, for a good while, fifteen minutes at least. Then – or when you come back from your walk – take a large piece of paper and draw your space. This is not a drawing of the physical space but the interior psychological space you found. If while you were in your space you felt limited or diminished, then draw a small space. If it was a large space – what the Bible calls 'a place of liberty' – 'He brought me into untrammelled liberty' (Psalm 18.19, REB) –

Discovery and acceptance of our Godspace sets us free to be, to believe and to act for others in a way which nothing else can do

then draw a large space. If it was joyful, colour it appropriately. If it threatened you, fill it with darker colours. If there were others present with you, then represent them in some way. If God was there, then find a way of indicating his reality. Reflect on it and then spend some time thanking God for that space and trying to see it as gift rather than threat. Ask yourself what relationship your practice of prayer has to that space. What is the language you use when in that space?

Such an exercise might enable you to see whether your practice of prayer is still too cerebral or too much of a series of requests and so still unrelated to an interior contemplative awareness of the reality of God, who fills all things.

Space and the mystical tradition

The writers of the Christian mystical tradition were very much aware of their Godspace. They believed that it was the point of entry, as it were; the point where it became possible for God to enter into our being and for us to become participants in the life of God. Dame Julian of Norwich, the English woman contemplative who lived and wrote her *Showings* in the fourteenth century, believed that the human soul can never be finally separated from God. She said,

> Greatly ought we to rejoice that God dwells in our soul; and more greatly ought we to rejoice that our soul dwells in God. Our soul is created to be God's dwelling place, and the dwelling of our soul is God, who is uncreated.

Dame Julian shared this understanding with Teresa of Avila, the Spanish mystical writer who lived nearly 300 years later. Saint Teresa speaks of the spring of water which arises in the depths of the soul. In *The Interior Castle*, her description of the journey of prayer, she speaks of two troughs of water which are filled in different ways, one by a series of mechanical aqueducts, the other from deep within itself. This silent spring within the soul, for that is what she is talking about, is a supernatural favour.

> God produces this delight with the greatest peace and quiet and sweetness within the very interior part of ourselves.

The writers of the Christian mystical tradition were very much aware of their Godspace

She reflects on Psalm 119.32 (which incidentally is also the source of Benedict's saying about running with hearts enlarged) and says,

> It seems that since that heavenly water begins to rise from this spring I'm mentioning that is deep within us, it swells and expands our whole interior being.

Another writer who developed this idea of interior space is, of course, the German mystic Meister Eckhart. Eckhart talks about the soul having a 'ground' and says that it is in this 'ground' that the word of God is born.

> That is what the text means with which I began: 'God has sent his Only-Begotten Son into the world.' You must not by this understand the external world in which the Son ate and drank with us, but understand it to apply to the inner world. As truly as the Father in his simple nature gives his Son birth naturally, so truly does he give him birth in the most inward part of the spirit, and that is the inner world. Here God's ground is my ground, and my ground is God's ground.

'God's ground is my ground, and my ground is God's ground'

Eckhart is heir to a tradition which sees the soul as a bride waiting to be completed by the arrival of the bridegroom, as a space within which God can act, within which the word, which is from the beginning, is spoken and so comes to birth. He knew about Godspace and asked people to wait, to remain in that Godspace with expectancy. It is interesting to discover exactly why Eckhart wrote in this way, because it has some relevance to our own religious concerns. Much of Eckhart's preaching was to the communities of women which the Dominicans had taken under their care as women's orders flourished in the thirteenth century. The growth of these communities represented what has been called 'vernacular theology'; they were places where new insights into the spiritual life could be found by those who were unable to aspire to belong to the clerical elite and so benefit from the education provided in the universities. The 'Béguinages', as they were called, were the best chance that women without a scholastic theological education could have. Eckhart spent a large part of his life preaching in and to these communities, usually in the vernacular, that is in German rather than Latin, and came to believe that finding one's ground in the depths of the Godhead, as he would have put it, was not dependent upon a scholastic theological education. He also became convinced that religious experiences of various kinds could often obscure our awareness of the reality of God. God was born within us when we allowed that birth to occur within us in secret, in ordinary, but also in the darkness of trust rather than in special experiences. Eckhart's view of poverty was a deeply radical one and involved a poverty of experience and a poverty of the will so that the word could be spoken and heard within us. One of Eckhart's phrases was that we had to learn 'to live without a why'.

The birth narratives

Perhaps you can now begin to see the relationship between the understanding of prayer that I am suggesting and the birth narratives in the New Testament. In each case, the people who are involved in the birth of Jesus are people who have been ready, who have already opened the inner ground of their soul and so are ready for the spring of life to well up from within, for the word of God to be spoken within them and so for the Incarnation of God to be released within their very beings. They are people who are prepared to allow God to live within them, prepared 'to live without a why'. Let us look at the different stories one by one.

In the first chapter of St Luke's Gospel we read two stories of annunciation: the story of the annunciation by the angel of the birth of John the Baptist to Zechariah and Elizabeth (Luke 1.5–25); and the story of the annunciation to Mary of the birth of Jesus (Luke 1.26–38). These two stories should be read together and compared one with the other. But first read the story of Hannah in 1 Samuel 1.1–28, for that story forms the background and it colours the telling of these two parallel accounts. In all three of the stories the characters involved display a simple emptiness. Hannah is barren, as is Elizabeth. Mary is a virgin. This emptiness is deeply important in the stories for it is remarked upon right at the outset. It is a lack. But it is also clear that it is a lack which is being held or borne by those afflicted and is not being put away or filled with some other consolation. Hannah goes to the Temple and, as it were, holds her emptiness to the Lord. The emptiness of Elizabeth is supported by her husband and both are said to be righteous before God, living blamelessly, patiently waiting for their lack to be filled or otherwise as God disposes. Into that emptiness comes a voice, or an angel representing a voice. A word is spoken. The word spoken to Hannah is that of Eli, who tells

The people who are involved in the birth of Jesus are people who have been ready, who have already opened the inner ground of their soul and so are ready for the spring of life to well up from within

her to go in peace for her petition has been heard. For Zechariah it is the angel standing at the right side of the altar of incense. For Mary it is even more directly a greeting. In all three stories the voice speaks a fertile word into the empty space of that person. The lack becomes a fertile space. In all three cases this lack is symbolised by the empty or barren womb and the conception of the child. In the stories of Hannah and Zechariah, this empty space within the person is also symbolised by the fact that the action is situated in the Temple, and in Zechariah's case not just the Temple but the holy of holies, the most secret innermost space where only the priest was allowed to go. The announcement that this innermost space is to be filled by the Word of God is greeted with an outpouring of song by Mary and Hannah. Zechariah, when he is able to speak, also sings God's praises.

In all of these stories, what comes to the fore is the utter graciousness of the event. The conception of the child is in all cases an absolute gift. This gift is 'spoken' by God in each of the characters. It is asked for; it is, to use language from Julian of Norwich, 'beseeched', but it is nonetheless gift. It comes when the person is open to whatever will be given. In the story of Hannah she hears the promise of God but then returns to her home in Ramah. From the way the story is told, she plainly has to let go of her claim upon God, simply to allow what is to happen 'to come to pass'. Once she lets go then the miracle occurs. With Elizabeth and Zechariah there is a similar atmosphere of acceptance. He is simply getting on with his job, following his roster, doing his turn, when, in the midst of everything else, the angel appears. As far as Mary is concerned the phrase 'and he came to her and said' picks up the same simple givenness of the event. It is a clear but unasked-for gift. In this way Hannah, Elizabeth and Mary become symbols of the human condition, simple, open, waiting with their lack, their emptiness, for God to give what it is he has to give. This is the beginning of prayer.

It should be said at this point that many will find it difficult to accept these women, described in these terms, as role models or as models for prayer. Surely, it will be said, women should be held up as active and strong, reaching out to co-operate with God in the search for justice in the world. Surely you have painted a picture of three meek, docile women just as men want them to be. If that is how we are supposed to be then I don't want any of it!

In all of these stories, what comes to the fore is the utter graciousness of the event

But it is not the meekness or the docility which is the point. It is, rather, the capacity to hear which the narratives emphasise. Each of these women has put herself in a position where she is able to listen, to attend to that which is not hers. They are obedient only in the original sense of that word, that is as 'hearers' of what may be given to them. They can hear what is said because their heads are not buzzing with things which are theirs. They have stayed with their lack rather than stuffing it full of things they think they need. Mary is not passive but still: still and attentive so that she may hear and co-operate with the word that is being spoken within her. But nor is it simply information that is imparted to Mary. She is not simply told about something that will happen and then left to decide what to do about it. The Word which is spoken is spoken in her and so involves her in its speaking. God's speaking is not an abstract speaking as that of a teacher imparting objective knowledge. The person spoken to becomes what is spoken. Mary herself becomes part of the word, the 'Godbearer', or, as some traditions put it, the *co-redemptrix*.

Before we go on to consider how these narratives relate to the life of prayer, it is worth remarking that the annunciation stories are not the only ones which speak of the filling of emptiness. Simeon and Anna appear when Mary and Joseph bring Jesus to the Temple to be presented to the Lord (Luke 2.25–40). Each of them is described in different ways as attentive. They are hearers, people whose inner ear has not been shut and who can hear the drums of God over and above the noise of this world. Simeon is described as 'righteous and devout, looking forward to the consolation of Israel'. Anna 'never left the temple' and once she had seen Jesus she began to 'speak about the child to all who were looking for the redemption of Jerusalem'. These phrases, 'the consolation of Israel' and 'the redemption of Jerusalem' are both deeply evocative phrases which indicate the lack or emptiness of those concerned, their expressed need for 'consolation' or 'redemption', but it is not a lack which is filled prematurely; it is a lack which is waited upon, loved almost, until such time as God answers the need which the lack expresses.

God's speaking is not an abstract speaking as that of a teacher imparting objective knowledge. The person spoken to becomes what is spoken

Prayer

Hannah, Elizabeth and Zechariah, Mary, Simeon and Anna are all models of the life of prayer. They are not such because they pray often or with many words but because they allow themselves to be hearers, people with an emptiness in their midst which they know must be filled, but also an emptiness which they know only God can fill in his own time and in his own way. They attend to the emptiness of God within them and await the birth of the Word of God within them. The accompanying metaphors of temple and womb, of being spoken to and listening, are all metaphors of the act of prayer.

Understanding prayer in this way will not be easy for some people because it will involve a shift in understanding. I think it is very clear that we need to recover a much deeper capacity to pray than we have at the moment, but we need to learn to pray in a 'mystical' manner. What I mean is that prayer is neither an asking nor a doing. To reduce it to such, as many contemporary manuals of prayer do, is to reduce it to the same status as anything else. It is to empty it of its quality of praise. Prayer is not simply another doing or asking, but with the simple distinction of being a 'spiritual' asking or doing. God is not so easily fooled. Prayer is not the same as everything else; it is a secret activity, something for which we must enter the innermost part of our being and then shut the door. We have to remember that, when the Word was gifted into their emptiness, Hannah and Mary burst into song. Essentially prayer is a form of song; it could even be described as a song which is continually being sung within us but with which we have lost touch, a secret song which God sings deep within the heart of all things. For prayer is not our asking but rather our appropriation of the asking and receiving which goes on between the persons of the Trinity. It is our appropriation of the divine life. It is what Julian of Norwich called a 'beseeching', the nearest human parallel to which is the 'beseeching' which goes on between the different members of a family or the two partners in a long and happy marriage. Prayer is not something we do but is something which is being done within us and within the whole creation by God, and we can either allow it or turn away from it. Prayer is a constant inner music which is playing within us and within the created order. We need to rediscover this music. There is within each one of us a space where this music can be heard, a silence within which it is played.

The mystical life is essentially a hidden matter. It is occasionally visible but it belongs properly underground, in hidden streams below the surface of our lives. It is a river deep within the rock of our being, coursing along in the

It is very clear that we need to recover a much deeper capacity to pray than we have at the moment, but we need to learn to pray in a 'mystical' manner

dark. It is a hidden music, a call sign secreted into the rich and abundant scoring of the great opera of life, a tune which occasionally bursts to the surface and makes its presence known. This mystical life is secret because it is of God. God is not seen except by his effects. He cannot be known entire. She is not experienced neat. He cannot be seen entire or all at once because she is God. To experience him neat would mean our annihilation. She simply is. And we resist this because we want to name her or to manage him or control her. But in matters of the spirit this is not possible. And that means that our prayer and our talk about God is inherently problematical, in a real sense 'empty', and must remain so. And we must be content with that. To be otherwise is to be an unbeliever.

The mystical life belongs properly underground, in hidden streams below the surface of our lives

Let not our souls be busy inns that have no room for Thee and Thine, but quiet homes of prayer and praise where Thou mayest find fit company; where the needful cares of life are wisely ordered and put away; and wide sweet spaces kept for Thee, where holy thoughts pass up and down, and fervent longings watch and wait Thy coming.

North India

The morning of joy

Don't hide;
Don't run,
But rather
Discover in the midst of life
A new way forward;
A Christmas journey
Sometimes marked by
Fragility and tears.

And on that road
To hold these hands
That even in their brokenness
Create a new tomorrow.
To dance at the margins,
And to see
The face of Christ
Within the beauty
and complexity
of our time.

To be touched anew
by this miracle
of Christmas;
God with us –
enfolding our journeys
on this morning of joy.
Transforming our vision,
healing our pain,
and
renewing, in love,
the slender, yet vibrant threads
of our devotion.

Peter Millar, Iona Community
Words for Today 1998 (IBRA)

God came down to us
like the sun at morning
wounded to the heart
by our helplessness.
Let us now depart
in his strength
to love and serve
one another.

Christian Conference of Asia